THINKING THROUGH ENGLISH

Open University Press

English, Language, and Education series

General Editor: Anthony Adams

Lecturer in Education, University of Cambridge

This series is concerned with all aspects of language in education from the primary school to the tertiary sector. Its authors are experienced educators who examine both principles and practice of English subject teaching and language across the curriculum in the context of current educational and societal developments.

TITLES IN THE SERIES

THINKING THROUGH ENGLISH

Paddy Creber

Open University Press
Milton Keynes · Philadelphia

Open University Press
Celtic Court
22 Ballmoor
Buckingham MK18 1XW

and
1900 Frost Road, Suite 101
Bristol, PA 19007, USA

First Published 1990

British Library Cataloguing in Publication Data

Creber, Paddy
  Thinking through English. – (English, language, and
  education series)
  1. Great Britain. Schools. Curriculum subjects: English
  language
  I. Title   II. Series
  420'.7'1041

  ISBN 0-335-09360-4

Library of Congress Cataloging-in-Publication Data

Creber, J. W. Patrick
    Thinking through English/Paddy Creber.
      p.   cm.—(English, language, and education series)
    Includes bibliographical references (p.).
    ISBN 0-335-09360-4
    1. English language—Study and teaching.   2. Thought and thinking—
  Study and teaching.   3. Language arts.   I. Title.   II. Series.
  LB1576.C775   1990
  428.4'07—dc20   89-48155
                                             CIP

Typeset by Rowland Phototypesetting Limited,
Bury St Edmunds, Suffolk
Printed in Great Britain by Biddles Limited,
Guildford and King's Lynn

To
Penelope, Mark and Felicity

No man can reveal to you
aught but that which already lies
half asleep in the dawning of your knowledge.
The teacher who walks in the shadow
of the temple, among his followers, gives
not of his wisdom but of his faith
and his lovingness.

If he is indeed wise he does not
bid you enter the house of his wisdom,
but rather leads you to the threshold
of your own mind.

(*The Prophet* by Kahlil Gibran, Heinemann 1978)

The great thing in Education is that each subject should make people's minds glow and become unsodden in a particular place, and when several glows have been fanned and set going, they may join up and the whole person becomes vividly alive and creative and afraid of nothing and unconscious of lower appetites and obstacles.

The work to be done in English is, above all, this. If any part of the programme doesn't seem to be doing this, think it out again and decide why it's there.

(*Teaching English* by G. Y. Elton, Macmillan 1929)

Pressures in schools created by the demands of examinations, the new National Curriculum and the regular testing of pupils encourages the tendency to place increasing emphasis on certain kinds of learning and the acquisition of specific skills. It can deaden creativity, neglect human and affective growth and lead to a somewhat lopsided education effort. That kind of distortion does not show up in examination results; its effects are felt later in emotional and spiritual deprivation . . .

(Cardinal Hume, quoted in *The Times* 4 January 1990)

Contents

Acknowledgements

Particular thanks are due to the following who read the manuscript at various stages of its development and offered encouragement and/or detailed advice: Conor Magee, Brian Merrick, Geoff Fox, Lesley Brooks, Denis Lawton, Andrew Stibbs, Richard Pring and David Evans.

Thanks are also due to the following for permission to reprint material quoted:

University of Chicago Press for the extract from *Yasnaya Polyana* in their *Tolstoy on Education* translated by Leo Weiner.

Routledge Kegan and Paul for extracts from Martin Buber's *Between Man and Man*.

Penguin Books Ltd. for two extracts from *The Language of Primary School Children*, by Connie and Harold Rosen.

Michael Benton and Geoff Fox for extracts from their *Teaching Literature, Nine to Fourteen*, Oxford University Press.

Gregory Harrison for his poem 'Alone in the Grange' from *The Night of the Wild Horses*, Oxford University Press.

Peter Lomas for the poem by the fourteen year old boy, quoted in his *True and False Experience*, Allen Lane.

Tony Buzan for material from *Use your Head*, BBC Books.

Faber & Faber for the poem 'The Play Way', *from Death of a Naturalist*, by Seamus Heaney.

Harlin Quist Books for six poems from *The Geranium on the Window Sill Just Died but Teacher You Went Right On*, by Albert Cullum.

General editor's introduction

I have to declare a particular interest in this volume which extends beyond the merely editorial function. In 1964 I was appointed as Head of the English Department at Churchfields Comprehensive School, West Bromwich; my immediate predecessor in that post was the present author, J. W. P. ('Paddy') Creber. He was leaving Churchfields to become a Lecturer in Education in the University of Manchester and, from there, he moved shortly afterwards to his present post in the School of Education in the University of Exeter. We have, therefore, been in close touch with each other's careers for a quarter of a century and I am delighted that the Open University Press was given the opportunity to publish the latest in Paddy's distinguished contributions to English teaching.

Churchfields was one of the very early purpose-built comprehensives and, while there, Paddy, like myself later, had to begin to define and devise methods for the teaching of English across the whole ability range. There were many voices engaging at that time with the same struggle, not least amongst them Holbrook and Dixon, both of whom have continued to make major contributions based on the experiences of the 1960s and beyond. Patrick Creber's first book in this field, *Sense and Sensitivity* (University of London Press 1965) grew directly out of his work at Churchfields and had a strong feel of the classroom about it. I had inherited his classes and could recognize amongst the desks in front of me many of the pupils about whom he wrote and whose work he quoted in what is still a remarkably fresh book on English teaching.

That book, like his subsequent work including the present volume, was characterized by a quality of intellectual strength, a sinewiness which might seem more appropriate to our present times than the so-called 'free-and-easy' 1960s. Indeed, both *Sense and Sensitivity* and *Thinking through English* go a long way to giving the lie to the parodies of progressive policies in education that have passed into the folklore (or demonology) of the popular contemporary history of education. These are points that the author addresses himself to in the first chapter of the book in a spirited defence of the best of 'progressive' teaching which, as he argues, has 'nothing soggy or sentimental about it'.

There is throughout, an insistence that schools exist to teach, or to provide secure environments in which young people have the opportunity to learn. Above all, there is a recognition that this process of teaching and learning is, in every sense, an intellectual activity. Hence, the ambiguous title of the present book.

English, language and literature, is itself a means of thinking and its processes need by us, as teachers, to be thought through. Much good teaching is a result of a reflective process. One is reminded of T. S. Eliot's comment on literary criticism, that 'first of all it is necessary to be very intelligent'. Those of us who, like Paddy and myself, have been much engaged over the years with both initial and in-service education for teaching are aware that the heart of any good teacher-education must be the encouragement of this reflective process, without which no short cuts or 'tips for teachers' will be of any avail. It is still not enough to ask 'What do we do on Monday?'; whatever we do must be based upon a rationale. It is such a rationale, built on his reflections upon a lifetime's professional experience, that Creber presents in this book. One may see some connections between its intellectual energy and that of his colleague at Exeter University, Robert Witkin, whose *The Intelligence of Feeling* (Heinemann 1974) similarly argues for the arts and the emotions as a way of knowing, an essentially intellectual activity.

The book is, therefore, in many ways unusally wide-ranging in its terms of reference. When I read the first version of the text I was struck by the range of reading that underscored its own thought. In particular it seems to me one of those rare books on teaching that have found something in the disciplines of psychology to turn to useful account. It is no accident that the references to the final chapter begin with Coleridge and end with Carl Rogers, whose work has clearly been a central influence on the evolution of Creber's own thought. But these are real psychologists with characteristic insights into the wholeness of the human heart. (Again one is reminded of yet a further pioneer in this same area of thinking about teaching English, Marjorie Hourd in *The Education of the Poetic Spirit*, now, regrettably, long out of print, which draws so widely and wisely upon Wordsworth as a key to educational processes.) It is far removed from the cultivation of measurement, the neo-behaviourism, of much that passes for educational psychology in the rather more meagre spiritedness of the present time. Hence the ironic sub-title to the introduction: *A core not a curriculum.*

This is, therefore, in many ways, and in the best sense of the term, an 'old-fashioned' book. While never losing sight of the issues and controversies of the present, it also affirms many traditional values in education, especially those associated with the intellect, with values, with personal growth and with responsibility. It is about 'standards' though it starts by affirming throughout that there are no easy means by which standards can be either measured or attained. The whole book stands as a powerful argument against many of the easy (and false) nostrums that are being peddled at the moment in the name of improving the quality of education. It deserves to be read as a reflective book on education in its own right, not just as yet another volume on English teaching. In this respect it makes an important and spirited contribution to the contemporary educational debate.

It would, however, be wrong to conclude this Introduction without pointing also to the help that it will give to the practising classroom teacher. 'What do we do on Monday?' is a question that still has to be addressed even if it has to be put in its place in the hierarchy of things. Each of the chapters contains wise summaries of practices that have proved to be of worth in the classroom; in particular I have found Creber's insistence upon the relationship between good English teaching and the teaching of art most helpful. Some of these ideas were worked out earlier in occasional publications of the School of Education in the University of Exeter, and it is good to see them re-worked here in a more permanent form.

Those of us who have worked alongside Paddy over the years will recognize a continuity in his thinking that enables the present book to be the distillate of the wisdom of a professional lifetime. Some of the poems he refers to, especially Scovell's 'The Boy Fishing' were in the filing cabinet I inherited at Churchfields and, new to me at that time, it went straight into my repertoire where it has remained ever since, even being included in one of my own early anthologies, *Loneliness and Parting*. It is good now to have a chance to acknowledge one's sources.

The phrase that comes finally to mind as an apt epithet for this book is that of E. M. Forster in *Howard's End* – 'only connect'. It is the inter-connectedness of things that is the real source of the 'thinking' indicated in Creber's own chosen title.

Anthony Adams

Introduction
A core not a curriculum

Education in Britain is extraordinarily like the weather: 'Brief spells of sunshine interrupted by showers or longer periods of rain.' Or wind. Or fog.

Helped by the witty inanities of people like Bernard Shaw (He who can, does. He who cannot, teaches), our culture has managed to maintain a deep scepticism about teachers and what they stand for. This has shown itself in predictable ways:

> Teachers have not only been inadequately paid, but care has not been taken to see that they are sufficiently supplied with the libraries and other intellectual opportunities which alone can keep them in the mental health and strength necessary for their task. (Newbolt Report 1921)

Though young teachers can still not afford even modest housing, things have of course changed. But how much, and how fundamentally? State education has always been a political issue and maybe it is even more so now than at the turn of the century. It is difficult, however, not to see similarities between the pressures upon teachers in those distant days and now. As Edmond Holmes, speaking of the period 1862–98, noted,

> For a third of a century 'My Lords' required their inspectors to examine every child in every elementary school in England on a syllabus which was binding on all schools alike. In doing this, they put a bit into the mouth of the teacher and drove him, at their pleasure, in this direction and that. And what they did to him they compelled him to do to the child. (Holmes 1911)

As I write, teachers, having survived the novel excitements of the GCSE examination, having partially digested the proposals for a national curriculum, and having wrestled with the implications of the Kingman (1988/9) Report, are mulling over the verdict of the Cox Committee (1988). As if this were not enough, they have just been informed that the GCSE is appropriate for only 80 per cent of the population and also that assessments based on 100 per cent coursework – very popular among English teachers – are no longer acceptable. Day by day, Holmes's words just quoted acquire new and more bitter relevance. Meanwhile over 25 per cent of them still have no appropriate training and 100 per cent of them feel underpaid and, even more importantly, undervalued.[1]

My concern is less with financial than with spiritual conditions. Shaw was wrong in his assumption that the teaching profession was the refuge of those not gifted enough to succeed elsewhere. Involvement over many years with English teachers convinces me that, given any reasonable circumstances, they show consistently high levels of inventiveness and commitment. While they need improved conditions of work and remuneration, in order to survive the latest assaults by the press, by the public, by parent governors or by politicians, what they need above all is *faith* – in children, in themselves and in their subject – the kind of faith that is close to that which impelled Holmes to write his book, in order, as he put it,

> to show that the externalism of the West, the prevalent tendency to pay undue regard to outward and visible 'results' and to neglect what is inward and vital, is the source of most of the defects that vitiate Education in this country, and therefore that the only remedy for those defects is the drastic one of changing our standard of reality and our conception of the meaning and value of life.   (Holmes 1911)

In 1990 credulous or uninformed observers might be forgiven for thinking that at last education is being taken seriously. They might easily be deluded by the cosmetic passion that informs the slogans now current – by all those beguilingly emotive words: 'professional responsibility', 'standards', 'excellence'. It is more sobering and more realistic to look back again to the Newbolt Report (1921).[2]

> However men may differ as to the relative importance of different objects in life, the majority are right in feeling that education should directly bear upon life, that no part of the process should be without a purpose intelligible to everyone concerned. . . . A quasi-scientific theory has long been accepted that the process of education is the performance of compulsory hard labour, a 'grind' or 'stiffening process', a 'gritting of the teeth' upon hard substances with the primary object not of acquiring a particular form of skill or knowledge but of giving the mind a general training and strengthening. This theory has now been critically examined and declared to be of less wide application than was thought. Its abandonment would do much to smooth the road of education, it would make it possible to secure for the child a living interest and a sense of purpose in his work, and it would replace the old wasteful system of compulsion and mere obedience by a community of interest between pupil and teacher.   (Newbolt Report 1921)

One hopes, without great optimism, that some of the current political/educational ideas, which often look very like *old* ideas, may also 'receive critical examination' and be found of 'less wide application' than has been assumed. What makes it all the more depressing, however, is that the knowledge needed to improve practice is already available. I share James Moffett's frustration:

> For the last twenty years, I have sought to help reform the language arts curriculum. During these twenty years, both applied research in training methods and basic research in verbal/cognitive processes have increased substantially. We now know

much more than in 1964 about how people use language and how they might be helped to improve their use of it. But more classroom innovation was taking place in the '60s than is taking place now in the '80s. And most of the advances made in that progressive era have been erased by regressive trends that began in the mid '70s. If greater knowledge leads to better action, why are most schools going backwards, retrenching into materials and methods long since tried and found untrue?[3]

Just how far one can draw parallels between the USA and Britain is open to argument and some of the curriculum practices cited are peculiarly American, but we ought to take very seriously his main contention:

Educators know far more about language learning than they enact, and many teachers are doing what they do not believe in, because they are not free. Resigned, or just glad to have a job, many usher their charges through an insultingly robotic reading program or grammar/composition textbook series that they despise and that even its own publisher scorns, all the while deftly plugging it into the tidy managerial systems and the back-to-basics mystique. Other teachers, wanting to believe in what they are told to do, try to rationalize; you don't think deeply about what you have no power over. . . . The current focus and reliance on research distracts us from the true causes of ineffectual and irrelevant methods of teaching. Partly, this preoccupation with research is a kind of whistling in the dark to keep up our courage.[4]

The references to Newbolt and Moffett are not just historically interesting or pleasingly exotic quotations. Wherever watchwords like 'rigour', 'professionalism' and 'excellence' are around there lingers the assumption that . . . somehow . . . things ought to be made tougher – not too far away, I think, from either the 'grind doctrine' alluded to by Newbolt, or the systematization of learning attacked as 'robotic' by Moffett. We may never have been as 'professional' as American educators, as keen on system and structure, but we have made the same mistakes – in perhaps a more engagingly amateurish way. We need however to watch out for the recurrent line of attack on new (twenty years, fifty years old?) developments, which labels them as 'progressive', mushily 'child-centred' (another term of abuse) and *laissez-faire*, lacking intellectual backbone.

For Moffett, for me and for many others on both sides of the Atlantic, the 1960s were an intellectually exciting time when to be young was, if not heaven, at least promising. Now popular mythology seeks to persuade us that it was an era of aberration. Thus Mr Oliver Letwin, who appeared in the late 1980s to have achieved some authority (hopefully brief and defying rational explanation) wrote in the *TES* extolling Mr Kenneth Baker's proposals for testing children's attainment and confidently cited resistance to competition as

another example of the sogginess of the sixties. The idea that the poor dears cannot bear too much reality is part of the sickly-sweet 'aren't we all doing wonderfully?' mentality that accompanied Britain's slide into mediocrity and insignificance. Mr Baker is attempting to reinstate the excellent – and about time too.[5]

In recent years I have seen abundant evidence of the connection between language and thinking,[6] and the implications this has for the classroom. What has hitherto eluded me is any evidence that recent or current ills derive from the widespread implementation of 'progressive' teaching methods. I am equally mystified by the apparent implication that large numbers of teachers have been spending their energies in the pursuit of mediocrity. Despite this, however, there is no doubt that Mr Letwin's line of thinking is pervasive enough to have daunted wavering spirits and to have closed some hitherto open minds.

Teachers need to grapple with serious issues, however, as well as with inane propaganda. To do this they must recognize and hang on to the new knowledge and insights that have indeed been achieved. Equally they must cling tenaciously to old truths. Secretaries of State for Education are pretty transitory phenomena and the likes of Mr Letwin mere shooting sparks in the educational firmament. They will, however, have their successors, who will keep up the same pressures. Despite these, the teacher who holds to both new and old truths and whose creed can incorporate, for example, the implications of recent research on language in the classroom as well as the inspired intuitions of Holmes (1911) and Sampson (1921) can, in small but important ways, alter 'what is' through a clear vision of 'what might be'.

Shifting educational pressures and emphases can be absorbed, accommodated or, where appropriate, ignored if teachers can discover, nurture and sustain a firm core of belief and conviction, a centre which *can* hold.

In this book I propose the *exploration and study of different ways of thinking* as offering such a core to the English teacher. It is not a book on method, but on belief; an idiosyncratic pulling together of strands gathered over thirty-five years, and testifying to my enduring conviction that the English teacher's lot may be, if not always happy, at least consistently interesting and utterly worthwhile.

As already suggested, emotive words do little to help teachers think about the job and they are hindered particularly by the current passion for what the Cox Report (1988) described as 'the false and unhelpful polarisation of views'. It's a long time since W. S. Gilbert suggested that we were either little liberals or little conservatives but teachers are now offered a wider choice. They may be progressive or traditional; informal or formal; language-based or literature-based; process-oriented or product-oriented; psycholinguistic or sociolinguistic; even (for those who like to think historically) they may be pre-Bullock or post-Bullock. Doubtless new choices will arise which, though equally unreal, will nevertheless produce the same anxiety. For most people the answer to the apparently urgent question 'Where do I stand?' is 'In the middle'. There are more important things to worry about than position-taking and my thinking is not much advanced by labelling myself 'slightly left of centre'.

A much more important anxiety is central and normal, however. This relates to teachers' attitude to teaching. Given the nature of their experience as pupil and student; given the amount of time they have submitted – with whatever degree of willingness or enthusiasm – to being taught, it is not surprising if they take a somewhat blinkered view of their own performance. In extreme cases their interest in 'teaching' may appear obsessive and the anxiety underlying this – the what-did-I-teach-today analysis – may well be reinforced by current moves to evaluate teacher performance. Such moves seem partly based on an assumption – re-emerging now that 1960s progressivism has been put in its place – that teaching is pretty much like putting a battery on charge, or dishing out appropriate doses of the 'right' medicine.

It is of course comfortable to assume that teaching is a logical business: if it doesn't work, increase the dose. I remember various textbook series which worked on this principle: Book 1: The Sentence. Book 2: More about the Sentence. Book 3: Still more about the Sentence. The notion that there is a traceable linear progression, which all 'professionals' should know, is comforting but – certainly as far as English is concerned – it is illusory, as the Cox Report (1988) recognized.[7]

In studying the use made of reading skills, for example, a Schools Council project sought to discover subskills and possibly a hierarchy of such skills. In vain:

> We conclude that individual differences in reading comprehension should not be thought of in terms of a multiplicity of specialized aptitudes. To all intents and purposes such differences reflect only one general aptitude: this being the pupil's ability and willingness to reflect on whatever it is he is reading.
>
> It should be added that this is not at all a case of the researcher setting out to prove a point and using statistics to justify whatever he wants to find. The reverse is true. With varying degrees of commitment, every member of the research team had embarked on the exercise with the aim of isolating the ultimate constituents of comprehension in the form of subskills. It is the data that proved resistant.[8]

There must be certain linguistic skills that are acquired before others but evidence of such order is generally too complex to form the basis for curricular proposals – English is an untidy subject! Taxonomies of Educational Objectives, such as that edited by Benjamin Bloom[9] and designed primarily to clarify thinking, have led to some inane misapplications at classroom level. One notes that Mr Letwin's support for Mr Baker's testing proposals derives from his belief in healthy or – in his word – 'realistic' competition. 'Realism' is a beguiling justification but competition generally means that somebody at the bottom of the scrum gets severely trampled on. In fairness to Mr Baker, I believe that his testing proposals were intended to improve diagnosis. Even there, however, a problem lurks: the knowledge that some people are starving more miserably than others does not, of itself, improve the situation. Nor does labelling a problem solve it.

In sum, I do not believe that English teaching, or thinking in English lessons, is primarily based on neat logical progressions. This may appear from the following three propositions:

1 *Good teaching is often deliberately unreasonable*
  Getting the right balance between sustainable (and comfortable) routine and unexpected challenge is hard. When the protests – Ooh, Sir! – suggest a blend of anguish and excitement, things are probably looking hopeful. In the passage quoted earlier (see p. vi) Gibran speaks of 'the teacher giving of his faith and his

lovingness'. The latter quality is that which enables the teacher to anticipate and to empathize; not least through his caring communication with the child in himself. It is a steady quality with nothing soggy or sentimental about it. Faith – which demands much rather than little – is given because teachers believe in the minds of their charges; because they bank on their capacity to meet challenges and in so doing surprise themselves.

2 *Good teaching has a strong element of interested experiment*
What happens when . . . ? What will happen if I . . . ?
Such experiment is based on knowledge but the teacher's stance is that of thinker rather than knower. In such modest, daily 'action research', progress is best evaluated not by the question 'What did I teach them?' but 'What did they (and I) learn?'

3 *Good teachers (quite) often don't (quite) know what they're doing*
This is obviously related to the previous proposition. It is a stance that can be maintained only through a good rapport with the teacher's class and an unobtrusively thorough degree of preparation.

The following chapters explore the implications of these propositions for those activities which normally fall within the scope of the subject called 'English'. The focus throughout will be on the kinds of thinking that normally occur, that may occur, that ought to occur, within the English classroom. Whether the immediate topic be oral, written, reading or dramatic activity, the aim remains constant – to help the pupil savour the excitement of thinking.

Notes

1 Bullock Report (1975) *A Language for Life*, London: HMSO, p. 228 and Kingman Report (1988) *Report on the Committee of Enquiry into the Teaching of English Language*, London: HMSO, p. 62. Cardinal Hume, quoted in the *Guardian*, (1990) 'Hume attacks schools act', 4 January.
2 It included F. S. Boas, Prof. C. H. Frith, J. H. Fowler, Sir Arthur Quiller-Couch, George Sampson, Prof. Caroline Spurgeon and J. Dover Wilson.
3 James Moffett (1985) 'Hidden impediments', in S. Tchudi (ed.) *Language Schooling and Society*, Upper Montclair, NJ, Boynton Cook for the International Federation for the Teaching of English.
4 ibid.
5 O. Letwin (1987). 'Testing issues', *Times Educational Supplement*, 18 September.
6 The relationship between the quality of Mr Letwin's thinking and of his language will be apparent.
7 Cox Report (1988) *English for Ages 5–11*, London: DES, p. 2 para. 1.8; p. 30 para. 7.5.
8 E. Lunzer and K. Gardner (eds) *The Effective Use of Reading*, London: Heinemann, pp. 63–4. They have a footnote on this point, citing parallel findings in an American study.
9 Benjamin S. Bloom (ed.) (1956) *Taxonomy of Educational Objectives, Handbook 1: The Cognitive Domain*, London: Longman. *Handbook 2: The Affective Domain* (1964) London: Longman.

1 Just thinking

When the mind is thinking, it is talking to itself.
(Plato)

The effect of social situations on thinking

In studies of children's language development children's questions occupy a considerable place. It wasn't perhaps necessary for parents to be told by psychologists that these were important: anyone with young children will know that children's questions are almost as much part of the parenting process as toilet-training. They are, however, somewhat less predictable, rather less easy to deal with, than nappies.

'Mum, what would happen if there were no more apples?'
'Why is 100 always more than 1?'

All parents can add examples of their own to these questions which stop you in your tracks. The late Al Read made splendidly humorous – and accurate – capital out of this aspect of childish behaviour and of inept adult behaviour in response.

The questions testify to the fact that the child is an awkwardly intelligent, sentient individual. As the language repertoire increases, so does the range of questions. Children arrive at school with a short but energetic and urgent span of experience behind them: for two or three years at least they have been preoccupied with making sense of things heard, felt, observed. They have been puzzling, connecting, guessing, explaining, remembering.

Though these activities are all very well, *per se*, schools – being institutions for numbers of people – are not easily able to cope with some of this behaviour. Intelligence is excellent, desirable, but questions (from thirty infants at a time) are something of a trial and may impede the process of getting the new recruits 'settled'. 'Sentience' is natural, but we don't want too much of it, and *individuality* can easily disrupt the whole process we're engaged on. This process indeed has much to do with quite other qualities – with conforming, behaving, fitting in. It is right that these should have a place, for they are to some extent a precondition for the tolerable functioning of an institution; moreover, the security and comfort of some rules and routines can, properly handled, enable children to recapture in a constrained setting some of the wild mental adventurousness that may have been natural to them in their home environment. That is, if they were lucky. Others, from homes where questions were too much of a nuisance to adults to be tolerable, may find some of the constraints of school quite familiar – if not comforting.

Pressures of socialization may increasingly preclude thinking, except along predetermined lines. Infants find in 'news' sessions – when, theoretically, all contributions from them are welcome and encouraged – that the teacher has particular views of what constitutes news and encourages some contributors but not others.[1] At the same time they may note that the teacher's language has surprising meanings. For example, when the teacher says 'I see', it generally means that she doesn't at all, or doesn't want to, or wishes that Johnny would shut up.

> 'The medium is the message' implies that the invention of a dichotomy between content and method is both naïve and dangerous. It implies that the critical content of any learning experience is the method or process through which the learning occurs. Almost any sensible parent knows this, as does any effective top sergeant. It is not what you say to people that counts; it is what you have them do. If most teachers have not yet grasped this idea, it is not for lack of evidence. It may, however, be due to their failure to look in the direction where the evidence can be seen. In order to understand what kinds of behaviours classrooms promote, one must become accustomed to observing what, in fact, students actually do in them. What students do in the classroom is what they learn (as Dewey would say), and what they learn to do is the classroom's message (as McLuhan would say). Now, what is it that students do in the classroom? Well, mostly, they sit and listen to the teacher. Mostly, they are required to remember. They are almost never required to make observations, formulate definitions, or perform any intellectual operations that go beyond repeating what someone else says is true. They are rarely encouraged to ask substantive questions, although they are permitted to ask about administrative and technical details. (How long should the paper be? Does spelling count? When is the assignment due?) It is practically unheard of for students to play any role in determining what problems are worth studying or what procedures of inquiry ought to be used.[2]

The message which Postman and Weingartner first promulgated in 1969 may seem familiar stuff but we do constantly need to remind ourselves of the unrealities of the classroom, of the amount of learning energy which is devoted to the 'hidden' as opposed to the ostensible curriculum. One suspects, moreover, that the title of their book, *Teaching as a Subversive Activity*, may, in the light of recent and proposed developments, re-assume a profound significance.

The unreality of teacher's procedures is something they also attacked with zest:

> It is not uncommon, for example, to hear 'teachers' make statements such as, 'Oh, I taught them that, but they didn't learn it.' There is no utterance made in the

Teachers Room more extraordinary than this. From our point of view, it is on the same level as a salesman's remarking, 'I sold it to him, but he didn't buy it'.[3]

In particular, since they were particularly interested in children formulating *their own* questions, the questions the teacher asks came under scrutiny. Again, familiar ground this, but one must not lose sight of the artificiality, *as perceived by the child*, of some of these questions. If one imagines the transference of a teacher-question to an out-of-school situation this becomes clear. You ask a man in the street,

'Could you tell me the time, please?'
'Five past ten,' he replies helpfully.
'Pretty good,' you respond with tempered pedagogic approbation.
'Four and a half minutes past, actually.'

Some of the pressures on the pupil are pleasantly suggested by Ted Hughes:

At school, I was plagued by the idea that I really had much better thoughts than I could ever get into words. It was not that I could not find the words, or that the thoughts were too deep or too complicated for words. It was simply that when I tried to speak or write down the thoughts, those thoughts had vanished. All I had was a numb blank feeling, just as if somebody had asked me the name of Julius Caesar's eldest son, or said '7,283 times 6,956 – quick. Think, think, think'.

(Hughes 1967: 56–7)

The potential damage attendant on some of these pressures, however innocent they may seem to the teacher, is suggested in the poem written by a 14 year-old boy as quoted by Peter Lomas:[4]

He always
He always wanted to explain things, but no one cared.
So he drew.

Sometimes he would just draw and it wasn't anything.
He wanted to carve it in stone or write it in the sky.
He would lie out on the grass and look up in the sky and it would be only the sky and
    the things inside him that needed saying.

And it was after that that he drew the picture.
It was a beautiful picture. He kept it under his pillow and would let no one see it.
And he would look at it every night and think about it.
And when it was dark and his eyes were closed he could see it still.
And it was all of him and he loved it.

When he started school he brought it with him,
Not to show anyone, but just to have it with him like a friend.

It was funny about school.
He sat at a square brown desk like all the other square desks and he thought it
    would be red.

And his room was a square brown room, like all the other rooms.
And it was tight and close. And stiff.

He hated to hold the pencil and chalk, with his arm still and his feet flat on the
floor, still, with the teacher watching and watching.

The teacher came and spoke to him.
She told him to wear a tie like all the other boys
He said he didn't like them and she said it didn't matter.

After that they drew. And he drew all yellow and it was the way he felt about
morning. And it was beautiful.

The teacher came and smiled at him. 'What's this?' she said.
'Why don't you draw something like Ken's drawing?
Isn't it beautiful?'
After that his mother bought him a tie and he always drew airplanes and
rocket-ships like everyone else.

And he threw the old picture away.

And when he lay out alone looking at the sky, it was big and blue, and all of
everything, but he wasn't anymore.

He was square and brown inside and his hands were stiff.
And he was like everyone else. All the things inside him that needed saying didn't
need it any more.

It had stopped pushing. It was crushed.
Stiff.
Like everything else.

For this boy, who shortly afterwards committed suicide, the constraints of school
– coupled no doubt with other pressures we know not of – proved too much. The
majority of pupils adapt, however, learning what to expect and what not to,
learning appropriate behaviours in each classroom and generally exhibiting a
remarkable submissiveness. The child in Albert Cullum's poem is philosophical
about the change school has wrought in him:[5]

I was good at everything
– honest, everything –
until I started being here with you
I was good at laughing,
playing dead,
being king!
Yeah, I was good at everything!
But now I'm only good at everything,
on Saturdays and Sundays. . . .

Boredom and absorption

If we are aiming at making the English classroom a place where the child can be 'good at things' – in particular at *thinking* – we need to recognize the

> subtlety and delicacy of the teacher's interchange with the student. A crude demand for effectiveness easily translates itself into a disastrous emphasis on externals simply because they are easier to get hold of than the central phenomena of insight and the growth of understanding. In an important essay of 1904, John Dewey distinguished between the inner and outer attention of children, the inner attention involving the 'first-hand and personal play of mental powers' and the external 'manifested in certain conventional postures and physical attitudes rather than in the movement of thought'. Children, he noted, 'acquire great dexterity in exhibiting in conventional and expected ways the form of attention to school work'. The 'supreme mark and criterion of a teacher,' according to Dewey, is the ability to bypass externals and to 'keep track of [the child's] mental play, to recognise the signs of its presence or absence, to know how it is initiated and maintained, how to test it by results attained, and to test apparent results by it.' The teacher 'plunged prematurely into the pressing and practical problem of keeping order in the schoolroom,' Dewey warned, is almost of necessity going 'to make supreme the matter of external attention.' Without the reflective and free opportunity to develop his theoretical conceptions and his psychological insight, he is likely to 'acquire his technique in relation to the outward rather than the inner mode of attention.' Effective classroom performance surely needs to be judged in relation to the subtle engagement of this inner mode, difficult as it may be to do so.[6]

I do not suppose my own early efforts were particularly 'subtle' or 'delicate'. Apart from a fairly normal concern with external control, they were certainly pragmatic: I noted above all what *worked* and tried to build on it; I noted also certain features of pupil behaviour when they were 'engaged'. In this I was, I believe, learning, as Dewey put it, to recognize 'mental play' when it occurred and was as excited by this as I was at other times bored with their boredom.

Three examples from this period are worth mentioning. The first – an attempt to explore and exploit things that they ought to be good at – sought to involve 11- and 12-year-olds in activities which demanded that they *pictured* and *remembered* aspects of familiar experience. I tried, by means of cross-reference to mime, to make imaginative concentration a comprehensible demand because a regular one. The particular process is described elsewhere,[7] but a similar approach was outlined by Ted Hughes (1967). He emphasized the need for concentration followed by writing like 'a hundred yards dash', the aim being

> to develop the habit of all-out flowing exertion, for a short concentrated period, in a definite direction.
>
> (Hughes 1967: 23)

and again

> The one thing to make sure of is that the topic be as definite as possible, and

preferably based on some specific memory. I doubt if much would come of just 'snow', as a subject. But there are an infinite number of categories within the general concept 'snow', and it is the teacher's job to help the pupil narrow the idea down to a vivid memory or fantasy.

(Hughes 1967: 39–40)

In work where they are called on to perceive, visualize and remember, it is difficult for pupils (and teacher!) not to become interested in the way different minds operate. Talking to children, Ted Hughes managed to convey this fascination:[8]

Now first of all I had better make it quite clear that I am going to talk about a certain kind of thinking. One of the odd wonderful things about this activity we call thinking is that to some extent everybody invents their own brand, has his own way of thinking, not only his own thoughts. You do not ever have to worry that you are not thinking properly – not unless you enter some very specialized job, where a very specialized kind of thinking is required. All you have to do really is think.

(Hughes 1967: 56)

If the teacher really can convey the message that they don't have to worry that they 'are not thinking properly', confidence and interest will grow.

This brings me to my second example. Early work of the kind described leads naturally into further explorations – of states of mind, tricks of the mind, and of associations. This last is a very rich and under-exploited area. Though many people think of 'butter' when asked for an association of the word 'bread', some may think of jam, others may make quite unlikely connections. The point about this is that it is not a matter of right or wrong; differences are not merely acceptable but fascinating subjects for further inquiry. With one class this led to an exploration of day-dreaming: how when you're bored in a lesson does your mind suddenly end up in the tropics? With renewed zest they studied the interesting quirks of Walter Mitty's mind. In all this we were finding 'recognitions' as we sought, in Ted Hughes's words, 'to catch those elusive and shadowy thoughts and collect them together and hold them still so that we can get a really good look at them!'

The third example is work with what was then called an 'early leavers' class'. Here, to vary the expected routine of writing unpromising letters to implausible employers, we spent a double period each week in a nearby youth centre's lounge discussing aspects of human behaviour – a sort of psychological rag bag: shyness and embarrassment; involuntary anger; inferiority complex. It was not well done but it taught me a great deal, especially how differently children will talk when removed from the setting they associate with boredom and failure and how often they can be trusted to sustain a discussion on their own. It also left me with the conviction that much material designed for such young people is infinitely patronizing. On the whole what they needed was not an idiot's guide to sex, parenthood or whatever, but a late night *adult* programme of the sort we might see on BBC2 or Channel 4.

I have cited these three examples not because they were intrinsically remarkable but because they represent the kinds of intuitive groping that a young teacher must be prepared to engage in. They stemmed from various intimations:

1 The difference between a class when it was bored and when it was engaged, absorbed, intrigued, outraged or excited.
2 Noting various things that appeared to 'work' fairly consistently.
3 An instinctive enjoyment of and belief in the mental capacities of children.
4 A vague sense of connection between different ways of thinking about and depicting life around us as represented in different media.
5 A belief, following Wordsworth, that rediscovering – and hence revaluing – the familiar was somehow central to the whole operation.

Early experience of this kind, however messy, eclectic, pragmatic and incomplete it may be, forms the foundation of the core of belief any teacher needs. In my case it enabled me with growing certainty and conviction, in Dewey's words, to 'recognise the presence of a child's mental play'.

'Mental play' in the classroom

The Play Way

Sunlight pillars through glass, probes each desk
For milk tops, drinking straws and old dry crusts.
The music strides to challenge it
Mixing memory and desire with chalk dust.

My lesson notes read: Teacher will play
Beethoven's Concerto Number Five
And class will express themselves freely
In writing. One said 'Can we jive?'

When I produced the record, but now
The big sound has silenced them. Higher
And firmer, each authoritative note
Pumps the classroom up tight as a tyre.

Working its private spell behind eyes
That stare wide. They have forgotten me
For once. The pens are busy, the tongues mime
Their blundering embrace of the free

Word. A silence charged with sweetness
Breaks short on lost faces where I see
New looks. Then notes stretch taut as snares. They trip
To fall into themselves unknowingly.

(Seamus Heaney)[9]

Heaney's wryly self-mocking account nevertheless directs us to signs that something significant is happening. In the first place there is the notion of the teacher, through the use of a classroom stimulus, exerting pressure, producing concentration. You can see the absorption, the concentration in the eyes' wide stare but more importantly in the fact that teacher has been 'forgotten . . . for once'. Because of this they are enabled, without self-consciousness or the coy consciousness of teacher-pleasing, to explore some recesses of their own minds.

Such things do not happen by chance, nor by the application of set recipes. Intuition, experience and empathy – which very much includes the capacity to anticipate reactions – all these are involved in the capacity to engineer situations in which new kinds of utterance – and hence of thinking – are made feasible. The teacher's role in this is something other than what is normally understood by the word 'teaching'; Postman and Weingartner even asserted that 'great strides can be made if the words "teach" and "teaching" are simply subtracted from the operational lexicon': the need was 'to invent a new term or name for the adult who is responsible for arranging the school learning environment'. It is difficult to see what this term might be, though I rather favour the word 'fixer'. The point is well taken, however: the teacher needs to pay less attention than hitherto to teaching and much more to arranging contexts in which things can happen. Thus the Cox Report (1989) when introducing programmes of study for speaking and listening, begins:

> Through the programmes of study pupils should encounter a range of situations and activities which are designed to develop their competence, precision and confidence, irrespective of their initial competence or home language.
>
> (Cox Report 1989: para. 15.25)

To arrange learning situations depends partly on strategies – to which I shall return – but primarily on the overall climate or atmosphere of the classroom. In attempting to create a facilitating climate we must – despite new exams, new curricula and new criticisms – hang on to the insights into the optimum conditions for classroom learning which have been gained in the past twenty years. The plain fact is that we now know enough to do better. We have learnt correctly to place emphasis on the acceptance and valuing of the child as an individual and more recently we have been helped in this by a new understanding of linguistic and social interaction within the classroom.

Critics of progressive English teaching have often argued that it is sloppy, results in an overvaluing of what the child produces and of social and personal as opposed to intellectual development. Their criticisms may be partly invalidated by the implicit assumption that what is needed is a return to the old rigour but this does not mean they contain no truth.

For children to be socially adjusted is not enough; for them to feel valued as persons is important, but not enough. In a learning situation they must do more than feel good about themselves; *they must quite specifically be led to feel involved in, and good about, the workings of their own minds* as they explore the excitement of thinking. 'Thinking' here is to be taken in a broad sense and will clearly include the recognition and exploration of feelings – infelicitously called by some the 'affective domain'. Involving the children in real learning brings with it a significant change in the feeling-tone of much of their work; they will not just think better but will also feel more fully and also more delicately. The cognitive and affective strands cannot usefully be separated.

All too often the early impact of schooling is negative, built up from very small apparent difficulties of the kind evoked in another poem by Albert Cullum:[10]

I have a messy desk,
I have milk money that rolls,
I have a lazy pencil,
a book that won't open,
a mouth that whispers.
I have a zipper that doesn't want to,
homework that won't work,
and a hand that throws crayons.
I have a shirt that's out,
shoelaces that won't tie.
And sometimes I wet my pants –
but never on purpose.

I remember a wise old nun who remarked, when I marvelled at the competence of the members of her infant class in using tape recorders, 'The only things these children can't do is what we teach them they can't do!' To change behaviour depends, first, on changing thoughts and feelings about oneself. The acid test of a school is not whether it turns out pupils who can perform particular operations but whether its pupils leave school with some positive conception of themselves *as learners*.

Our attempt must therefore be to create an appropriate climate, recognizing the constant interaction between social and intellectual growth; between context and competence. By way of example, consider the evident numerical competence of average darts players in their local pub and contrast this with their previous customary performance as pupils in a lowly GCSE or non-examination maths set. The most significant thing about the numerical wizardry of darts players is that they perform like this *when they are playing*.

Developing a thinking climate

In the creation of an effective classroom climate for thinking, there are many factors to be considered; at this point I shall, however, concentrate on just one: *Questions* . . .

In *Teaching as a Subversive Activity*, Postman and Weingartner (1969) sought to promulgate a curriculum based on a version of the inquiry method. Some parts of their argument, or perhaps the rather confident (and American) tone, may now appear a little dated; certainly one balks a little at some of the aphorisms –

'Meaning is in people', for example. Despite this the central message is as relevant today as in 1969:

> Once you have learned how to ask questions – relevant and appropriate and substantial questions – you have learned how to learn and no one can keep you from learning whatever you want or need to know.[11]

A slightly more tempered and more profound view of the matter, taking into account some real problems, is found in Richard Jones's *Feeling and Fantasy in Education.*

> Teachers know that the proofs of well-composed and conducted lessons are more often found in the questions raised than in the answers given. Moreover, one has only to spend some time as a professional outsider in an elementary school to know that children will share their answers with almost anyone who asks the right questions; but they will only share their questions with their own teachers – and then only if they love them. After all, there is little risk in giving an answer, it is either right or wrong and that is usually the end of it. But to share a question is often to invite inspection of one's tenderer parts. Like other loving acts this is not something we do with strangers.[12]

The best elaboration of these ideas about love and trust, as part of the climate that we seek to establish, comes in a book which remains a source of wisdom and inspiration – Martin Buber's *Between Man and Man* (1947). In his chapter on the education of character he argues that 'there is only *one* access to the pupil; his confidence'. He goes on:

> to the adolescent who is frightened and disappointed by an unreliable world, confidence means the liberating insight that there is human truth, the truth of human existence. When the pupil's confidence has been won, his resistance against being educated gives way to a singular happening: he accepts the educator as a person. He feels he may trust this man, that this man is not making a business out of him, but is taking part in his life, accepting him before desiring to influence him. And so he learns to *ask.*
>
> (Buber 1947: 135)

and later:

> Confidence, of course, is not won by the strenuous endeavour to win it, but by direct and ingenuous participation in the life of one's pupils – and by assuming the responsibility which arises from such participation. It is not the educational intention but it is the meeting which is educationally fruitful. A soul suffering from the contradictions of the world of human society, and of its own physical existence, approaches me with a question. By trying to answer it to the best of my knowledge and conscience I help it to become a character that actively overcomes the contradictions.
>
> (Buber 1947: 135)

Teachers do not too easily invoke concepts like love and trust as characteristics of the environment they are trying to create any more than pupils normally admit to loving their teacher. Yet though not overtly expressed, such qualities are there in some measure wherever there is the openness that mutual confidence brings; wherever there is a good combination of intellectual strenuousness and mental play. Moreover, if you do not deal in love, trust and confidence what chance have you of persuading the defeated adolescent to try again? As if to complement all this, Anatole France had a lighter and terser formulation:

'It is only by amusing oneself that one can learn.'

(Quoted in Purves 1972)

The idea loses something in translation since the activity proposed is not quite so smugly self-centred as it sounds; 's'amuser' properly carries also the sense of *playing*, even of 'messing around'.

I believe that the teacher's aim should be to promote this messing around: the range of possibilities is enormous, as this short list may suggest:

introspective play	guessing play
reflective play	associational play
memory play	logical play
nonsense play	listening play
verbal play	looking play
vocal play	
repetitive play	narrative play
	mime play
	role play
	kinesic play
	spatial play

While the possibility of making mental play central to English teaching depends primarily on the classroom climate, it can also be fostered or inhibited by specific 'teaching' strategies. Generally these will be considered under the activities dealt with in succeeding chapters but certain preconditions may be mentioned here.

In the first place, there is the physical environment. Many of the most effective strategies depend on the availability of flexible space so that different group-ings are possible appropriate to different tasks. The Bullock Report (1975) exam-ined the needs of an English department and concluded that these were just as specialized as those more commonly recognized for science or modern languages.

One of the side-effects of the notion that 'Every teacher is a teacher of English' has been its extension to 'Any room is suitable for English'. Many heads to whom we spoke recognised the fallacy of this assumption and took great pains to avoid it when drawing up the room timetable. In some schools, however, it was obvious that English was deemed to have no requirements that could not be answered by any classroom that happened to be free.

. . . a substantial proportion of English teachers – over one third – are itinerant within the school, carrying their books about with them from one lesson to another. Even where they have the use of a regular room for their English lessons, this is by no means necessarily one designated as an English room. Thus, many teachers are unable to establish an environment in which they can exhibit work, put up illustrations and posters, mount displays and models, etc. We regard this as unsatisfactory, and believe that all English teachers should have the stability that is so essential to the kind of work we envisage.

. . . In our visits to schools rarely did we see pupils with the space to spread their papers, or the degree of 'psychological insulation' for individual reading and writing that adults would expect for themselves. Group work requires the space to allow tables and chairs to be re-arranged into clusters. Discussion operates best when the pupils are sitting round a group of tables or in a horseshoe of chairs. These examples alone – and they are chosen as the most obvious – indicate how important to English teaching is generous space. The first essential is for the flexibility which allows the teachers a number of options. It should be possible for a teacher to spend a major part of his time in his own base. It should also be possible for a group of teachers to share a cluster of spaces which are adapted to the needs of varying activities and varying numbers of pupils. . . .

(Bullock Report 1975: 232–4)

The case for proper provision for English which the Bullock Report laid out clearly and moderately remains largely ignored and the notion persists that all the English teacher needs is a number of desks, blackboard and chalk. The absolutely debilitating inadequacy of such provision has been thrown into even sharper focus by the experience of teachers trying to teach for the new GCSE examination with its emphasis on oral competence, self-evaluation, co-operative work, and so on. The disenchantment which leads English teachers to leave the profession has at least as much to do with these problems as with pay, or the difficulties of discipline. Those who endure continue to perform miracles in the teeth of adversity.

The other preconditions relate to the proper understanding of the kinds of structures which apply in children's natural play: the extent to which their games are quite disciplined ways of messing about and the need to recreate in the classroom the same blend of rule-structure and the support this affords. Thus children may be comfortable enough to respond to challenge and to allow their minds to be engaged.

The actual techniques employed are too numerous to mention here but most will involve the kinds of 'fixing' or arranging referred to earlier and their efficacy will largely depend on an appropriate combination of grouping and task. Part of the essential 'engineering' lies in manipulating the social situation to accord with the kind of language work to be attempted. The task itself – addressed to individuals, pairs, small groups or whole classes – is a crucial element in the situation. The particular context in which we expect it to be accomplished will largely determine the range and quality of feasible response by the pupils. Indeed the *meaning* of the task may often be said to depend on this context.

Notes

1 See S. Worster (1985) 'When news is bad news: two contexts for infant narration', in *Perspectives 19: What are English Teachers for?*, School of Education, University of Exeter.
2 N. Postman and C. Weingartner (1969) *Teaching as a Subversive Activity*, New York: Delacoste Press, p. 19.
3 ibid. p. 37.
4 P. Lomas (1973) *True and False Experience*, London: Allen Lane, pp. 94–5.
5 A. Cullum (1971) *The Geranium on the Window Sill Just Died but Teacher You Went Right On*, New York: Harlin Quist.
6 Sheffler (1968) 'University scholarship and education of teachers', in *A Record-Teachers College*, p. 9, quoted in Courtney B. Cazden (1972) *Child Language and Education*, Eastbourne: Holt, Rinehart & Winston, p. 137.
7 See J. W. P. Creber (1965) *Sense and Sensitivity*, University of London Press, pp. 87–90, or revised edition (1983), School of Education, Exeter University, pp. 90ff.
8 As the tone makes clear the book was based on talks to children, in a remarkable series called 'Listening and Writing', devised by Moira Doolan for the BBC Schools Department.
9 From Heaney (1966) *Death of a Naturalist*, London: Faber, p. 56.
10 Cullum, op. cit.
11 Postman and Weingartner, op. cit. p. 23.
12 R. Jones (1968) *Feeling and Fantasy in Education*, London: University of London Press, p. 47.

2 Talking and thinking

Chapter 1 examined some general factors which constrain or encourage the pupil's thinking and the need to create the right climate for mental play within the English classroom. This chapter addresses the first of those specific aspects of English which occupy the rest of the book. After a brief consideration of relevant evidence from psychology and psychotherapy the chapter will concentrate on situations and techniques which facilitate playful thinking in talk.

The recognition of the importance of talk is undoubtedly the major advance in the subject in the past twenty years. Given however that this recognition is by no means universal it has been particularly heartening to have the importance of talk and listening so unequivocally emphasized by the report of the Cox Committee. We are however some way from agreement on precisely how teachers should be prepared for this aspect of their work. Many official reports have found teacher training an easy target for criticism, often formulated in such terms as 'Unless students have been taught/know about X they are inadequately prepared.' More recently there is an increasing tendency towards something more prescriptive: 'Students should have undertaken not less than Y hours of study on this subject.'

Of late, in the preparation of English teachers, the attention focused on language has been often expressed in such terms, as if it were all a matter of correct dosage. While courses which never mention crucial concepts may clearly be judged inadequate by any standard, the underlying preoccupation with 'knowing' and 'being taught' remains disturbing in this context. One is reminded of Tolstoy's ironic portrait:

A teacher from a German seminary, who has been instructed by the best method, teaches by the Fischbuch. Boldly, self-confidently he sits down in the classroom, – the tools are ready: the blocks with the letters, the board with the squares, and the primer with the representation of a fish. The teacher surveys his pupils, and he already knows everything which they ought to understand; he knows what their souls consist of, and many other things, which he had been taught in the seminary.[1]

As life becomes more complex, the list of things the teacher should be taught at the seminary grows longer; just now word-processors are clamouring for attention. But the problem is not of this kind, certainly not as far as the current topic is concerned. The effective handling of talking and thinking in the classroom depends on qualities of human resource not normally addressed, let alone developed, in the training process.

This is why some of the most important writers have gone outside the fields of literature and language in order to support their thinking. A particular source of insight has been psychology, whether analytic or therapeutic in stance. In recent years the works of Simon Stuart and David Holbrook come to mind as showing this influence. The work of their precursor, Majorie Hourd (1949), is often neglected by comparison: she combined literary and psychological insight to a degree they couldn't match but in consequence she is a less racy read, her profounder and more scrupulous understanding less easily shared.

Without claiming any such expertise, I would want to acknowledge my own debt to her and to the work of such as Erich Fromm, Carl Rogers and Abraham Maslow. Also – in the related field of art – to Herbert Read and Marion Milner. All this work points in a quite different direction from what is normally suggested or implied by critics of teacher training. Witness the following from D. W. Winnicott, in which please read *English teacher* for 'therapist' and *pupil* for 'patient'.

> psychotherapy is done in the overlap of the two play areas, that of the patient and that of the therapist. If the therapist cannot play then he is not suitable for the work. If the patient cannot play, then something needs to be done to enable the patient to become able to play.

> (Winnicott 1971: 54)

I do not want to push the parallels too far; certainly, for Winnicott, 'play' has particular meanings in a particular context. The spirit is right, however, and in such works there are often points of contact more suggestive to the teacher, and often wiser, than in books on teaching method. If our meeting with children is to be educationally fruitful, as Buber suggests, it has to be a real meeting. If pupils' energy is spent guessing at what's in the teacher's mind this may be unfruitful. If, however, the teacher can enjoy something of the same game, guessing at what's in the pupils' minds, talking and thinking can really happen.

Contexts and techniques which facilitate playful thinking in talk

Arnie sat in the circle of six students, looking reflectively at the plywood Jokari bat he held in his hands. He was retelling the story of the Trojan horse, from a somewhat novel viewpoint. He told of the pain the horse felt at each stage of its construction, of the tearing agony of the saw, of the wearing weight of the cross beams and of the sharp, fierce stab as each nail was driven into its frame. Other groups in the room stopped to listen in; his own group was rapt. 'Finally,' he said, 'it was nearly complete but so far from relief the only thing it felt was the accumulated burden of pain.' He looked at the bat again, fingered it gently, then slowly lifted it handle upwards. 'As the last nail was driven in, the horse's control broke. And it shed a single, wooden, tear . . .' He looked solemnly round the group. 'This is that tear.'

This was probably the most memorable individual effort in a game I have often played with teachers, students and older pupils. Its particular virtue is as an ice-breaker in early work with a group: Arnie's group of PGCE students were meeting for the third time. The game also constitutes an excellent reference point for later work on such things as story-telling.

The framework of the game is simple. In groups of five or six they are told that they are all *experts* appearing on a television antiques programme. Various models are quoted, including the one from which I borrowed the name for the game, 'Patently Obvious'.[2] The task of each individual in turn is to talk expertly for about three minutes about the object which is given to them, which can be attributed to any period of history, including the future. The challenging constraint is that the object can be anything *except what it really is*. Simple, everyday objects are best – such things as dustpans, brushes, board-rubbers, teapots.

In a sense, the game is unreasonable, at least in its manner of presentation. There is no time to prepare as an object is produced 'out of the hat', given to one member in each group who, while handling it, is expected to start talking immediately and after three minutes to pass it on to a neighbouring expert, who will, of course, have a different opinion. It is sometimes better if experts are allowed to question each other's interpretation. I have not known the game to fail with any group of teachers and only very rarely with an individual, though it should not be the first activity undertaken and hence groups would come to it slightly 'warm'.

Its success seems to derive from four features in particular. First, the unreasonableness already mentioned seems to offer the right level of playful challenge. Second, the organizer's act of faith is crucial, conveying a confident expectation that they can do it, that they can be inventive, that they can play this kind of game. Third, the game generally produces a good deal of laughter, often of an admiring sort. Fourth, the structure of the game is manageable, providing support through

1 its routine
2 its speed
3 the familiarity of the expert 'voice' they are required to imitate
4 perhaps most important, the 'prop', here very aptly named. The object, or more particularly the handling of the object, facilitates talking while thinking and also makes pauses natural and bearable. Often an object elicits 'acting' from people who would normally claim to be frightened of *drama*.

The point about objects as supports for thinking reminds me of Mulligan. Mulligan was a small, rather pallid and skinny youth, who somehow engaged sympathy and even affection despite a capacity for villainy which all recognized but which schooling had as yet managed to keep in precarious check. His last year coincided with early attempts to translate ideas about 'oral English' for the then new CSE into practice. This subject was still obscure, if not alien, but somehow 'talks by pupils' were judged appropriate. One afternoon Mulligan, whose obdurate taciturnity could normally be counted on, astounded me by talking about judo with fluency and ease for three-quarters of an hour. Holding up items of his kit, he explained their design and function, then he went into the major principles of the art and finally he invited and dealt with many interested questions from his peers. If I was surprised by this *tour de force*, it was not only because of his departure from normal behaviour but also because the week before, having agreed to talk, he had stood miserably dumbstruck until released by me from a situation which embarrassed us all. At the end of that lesson one of his mates, who had not enjoyed it and knew that I hadn't, paused on his way out. He did not need to tell me I could have handled it better; he just said – 'Next week, sir, get him to bring his kit.' To the wise, certain things are obvious. If you are a teacher, things are often obvious afterwards.

Both Arnie and Mulligan were instances of individuals responding to a challenge in a facilitating atmosphere and supported by 'props'. Before looking at some more general issues and principles it seems appropriate to describe another exercise which has a strong element of challenge and which I particularly enjoy using with PGCE students. This was specifically designed for a group of kindred spirits, members of a commission I was running at a NATE conference on 'The role of play in English teaching.' Because I was to be working with (if not preaching to) the converted, I sought to design an exercise that would be an act of faith in the consumers, would be highly structured, yet thoroughly arbitrary and unreasonable. It was very much a 'let's see what happens if' exercise.

It remains in pretty much its original form and runs as follows. A group is divided as randomly as possible into pairs, though there may be some attempt to balance the sexes. Each pair is instructed to write down an interesting word or phrase – quickly. This is to be passed on to the next pair, round the circle. The word or phrase is to be a starting-point for those receiving it, who then have to follow this procedure.

1 Write a five-minute dialogue. One hour allowed. The word or phrase received is to be used just as a starting-point and its associations canvassed, but need not be used.
2 After an hour a script is duplicated and handed over to the next pair in the circle. This needs to be worked out beforehand – they need to know for whom they are writing. It may happen also that with uneven numbers one pair will be

writing for a threesome (who will have had to do stage 1 together), in which case an extra copy of script will be needed.
3 The pairs, armed with their scripts – allow half an hour for the hand-over – have a further hour to rehearse and interpret their scripts. They are instructed not to rewrite disliked scripts but to use devices such as pauses, 'business' and even mime to flesh them out. They should not try to learn scripts but make them as unobtrusive as possible.
4 The scripts are performed in front of the audience, the authors and the starter word being acknowledged before each presentation.

Again, the game was deliberately designed to be challenging to a group who had consented in advance to play. Despite this it works consistently well with 'pressed men' on a PGCE course. Not merely this, but my initial tendency to delay its introduction till late on in the first term has been modified as my own faith in the students has grown. I now tend to use it as soon as possible: after perhaps four or five weeks because, like all such challenges, if it can be successfully met it raises morale and galvanizes commitment, particularly important considerations given the brevity and concentration of the PGCE course. Quite basically, the aim is to give groups the opportunity to surprise themselves and the sooner this boost can be given, the better. After the presentations there is only applause, no evaluation, but students are encouraged to reflect on the *processes* involved in the exercise, which parts they most enjoyed and which they found most difficult.

We have looked at three situations, two of which have a strong game element and which are indeed highly 'contrived'. I would not want to suggest that the English curriculum is dependent on an inexhaustible supply of games, however, but I hope that these examples, by being concrete, may first convey the spirit of the endeavour and second, perhaps, suggest other possibilities. I would also want to play down the element of contrivance at the same time as pointing out that however good the climate, however effective we are, the classroom remains an *unnatural* place.

Climate depends very little on gimmicks, however, and very much on the pursuit of relationships that are as natural as possible within the institutional constraints. The essential point is again made in a poem by Albert Cullum:[3]

On the mornings you tell us about the night before,
you're like one of us.
The dress you bought,
or a movie you saw,
or a strange sound you heard.
You're a good storyteller, teacher, honest!
And that's when I never have to be excused.

Story-telling as an art is at last beginning to receive serious attention, even to find a place in teacher education. Coupled with this is the more humdrum use of personal anecdote through which the teacher – as the child in the poem asserts –

can establish the right kind of reciprocal relationship with those taught. In a climate, moreover, where anecdote is thinkable it is also infectious: children naturally follow teacher's lead. And being allowed to tell anecdotes reinforces the sense of self, confirms in the child's mind the hopefully emergent notion that teacher does listen, is interested, does value the child's experience and thinking.

In this connection, I recall with particular gratitude the example of Leila Godrich, a teacher working in an EPA (educational priority area) school with a class of sixteen under-achieving or problematic 8-year-olds. The core of her work was story. She had two main strategies – story projects shared with whole class and individual stories told to one other child, who also recorded them, these being later made into booklets to be read by members of the class. Something of the atmosphere on which everything depended is caught in a transcript of a discussion before they began a project which was to occupy them happily for the whole of the second term.

Teacher: Now! Do you remember we talked about making our own little families and then writing our own books? Oh good. Well, I think we will be able to start this afternoon.

Colin: We'll need a lot of boxes.

David: Frank brought some. He's always bringing boxes.

Mark: Well, I brought a box as well. Miss Godrich, didn't I bring a box? My box is my house. I'm going to live in my box.

Teacher: Whoever you like can live in your box. Just think, you can make as many people as you like to live in your box. It will be yours and you can choose and there will be nobody to tell you what you can do. It will be like having your own little world.

Henry: And God's.

Teacher: I beg your pardon?

Henry: And God's. Nobody can have a world without God in it.

Teacher: Who else will you have?

Henry: I'll have a gang of ten children and they can fight.

Teacher: That's a lot of little people to make.

Henry: Yes. I'll only have six perhaps.

David: I know who's going to live in my house. I'll have the Green family and they live in Green Cottage.

Teacher: And where is Green Cottage? Is it in a village or a town? Is it by the sea or in the country?

David: It's in a village and it's called 'Our World'.

Teacher: That's a funny name for a village.

James: No it isn't. It's good. You said it was our world. Didn't she say it was our world?

Henry: And God's.

Teacher: All right. 'Our World' it shall be, and we'd better start building it this afternoon, or else it will never get finished. . . .

In subsequent lessons the project gained momentum; here for example is David in full spate:

> My family is going to be called the Green family and we've got a Mummy and a Daddy and a baby and the baby is 1 and the Daddy is 55, and the Mummy is 62. And they live in a house with white curtains and a white door and they got a white cat and they got a blue – no – they got a brown dog and two little rabbits in a cage and they got a table with a carpet over and they got a table with cups, silver cups and silver plates and they got a living-room with a big settee and the colour is brown all their furniture is brown and they got a bar and they got some plants and they got lots of things.

To this characteristically, and importantly, Miss Godrich replies:

> Well done! Thank you! They are rich then, your family, with all those silver cups and saucers.

Just as, later on, she responds to Frank's proposed names for his family's fish:

> Laurel and Hardy, the fish? That's clever. Thank you, Frank.

During this phase there was also much general discussion, for example,

> about what a village needs: church, hospital, shops, school etc. As the model grew, the children began to move their houses around the village, deciding where to live, who will be neighbours, etc. – a great deal of good discussion.

By the end of a month, Miss Godrich noted in her log

> discussions about the siting of an airport!

The early stages of construction seem to me to have been important in two ways. First, the modelling provided an activity through which ideas could be incubated, rather as can happen in mime and drawing. Second, there was a lot of social talk leading to co-operation: at the end of the first week the teacher noted:

> The children are already beginning to form groups – two are making a pair of semi-detached houses, and two are sharing a 'rug shop' (inspired by bits of sheepskin). The father figures are being given jobs – milkman, shopkeepers, a vicar.

As the routines associated with the class project became more comfortable, Miss Godrich sought to encourage individual story-telling. Something of the progression that took place can best be conveyed by the details of her own notes.

> *Mon. 24th January*
> Began a rough copy of individual family booklets – children very excited at this stage, and not very good.

> *Tues. 25th January*
> Using the children's rough copy and the taped conversations, I began to build up the stories with the children. They told the story, I wrote it down.

> *Wed. 26th and Fri. 28th January*
> I continued with this work as the children worked on their models, and began to

illustrate their stories. Unfortunately the paper used (duplicating paper) won't take felt tips, so the pictures will have to be done separately and stuck on later.

Mon. 31st January
I taped the stories today to save time but the children are far less fluent than when they are just talking to me. Obviously the tape recorder is inhibiting. A pattern is emerging in the stories, in their use of language. So far no adjectives have been used except for nice(!), big, and little (by far the most popular).

Half-term 11th – 21st February
The model is now complete. Or rather there is no room for any more, as it covers three large tables and takes up almost a quarter of the teaching area! This half-term I do not intend to devote set times to this work but to let the children tell their stories in their own free time. I will put the tape recorder in a corner, show them how it works, let them form their own groups and see what happens.

Tues. 1st March
The children are quite happy with the new arrangements and are working together very well. The two groups who have already recorded their stories, (1) Billy and David, (2) Eric, Colin and Andrew, have done so with great confidence.

Thurs. 3rd March
I have used a transcription of the group 2 story as a basis for talking to those children to try to get a more balanced version as they become rather excited and incoherent on the tape. The group 1 children were very clear, with a well-balanced story which was typed verbatim.

Wed. 9th March
Group 3: Mark and Henry recorded a lovely story with a nice interplay of characters helping each other. This second series of stories seem to be much more fluent and far less fragmented.

Thurs. 10th March
Frank, in Group 4, and Ken, told his story 'The Rascals come to town', with great 'expression' and obviously enjoyed himself. This pleased me as he is a very quiet child, and rather withdrawn. This story needed discussion with the children. They saw that they had only given an outline of a story on tape, and enthusiastically filled in the gaps.

Wed. 16th March
We taped a book together 'Spring in our World': the children are no longer worried about the tape recorder and I think we are now getting a much better quality of language – certainly more of it. It is interesting to note that the children's written work is improving, and they are now beginning to write stories with a middle as well as a beginning and an end.

I had to ask Ann and Carol to tell me their story so I could write it down as Carol's speech is so poor I could not transcribe it from the tape.

It is impossible to convey the sea-change wrought in the lives of these children. After another term, partly devoted to tracing the adventures of Fred, a massive dragon which hung from the ceiling, the classroom boasted a library of well over 100 homegrown titles. And they had been read. That at any rate lies at the heart of the change.

I have seen other teachers getting children to write books for themselves or other children, of course, but their efforts, even where successful, were half-hearted by comparison. What was remarkable about Miss Godrich's work had little to do with the originality or otherwise of the strategies used but everything to do with the conviction, consistency and coherence which marked their application. Her work is particularly interesting to me in its blend of 'climate' and facilitating structure.

Structures can easily be devised which emphasize weakness, and teachers whose main preoccupation is with control or discipline have specialized in these for years. The challenge, however, is to facilitate both thinking and utterance through the structures used. We are aiming through our knowledge of factors which inhibit performance to find contexts which will (to go back to an earlier example) enable the darts player to operate at levels of maximum competence, in fact, to *play*.

Some structures have been designed specifically to facilitate thinking and have particular relevance to aspects of English teaching. Despite a certain commercial flavour in their presentation and dissemination the ideas of Edward de Bono demand attention. To take two examples, his unit called PMI (Plus, Minus, Interesting) involves children in producing and roughly sorting ideas in response to some challenging statement such as 'Should children be allowed to divorce their parents?'[4] The use of the technique, which has firm ground-rules, is clearly relevant to various kinds of discussion work (including the written mode) in which it is hoped to involve all the class through a feasible initial task (or game). It also contains the much underused technique of brainstorming where, for a short burst, participants are to produce ideas pell-mell without stopping to evaluate or analyse, which processes may, however, constitute a useful subsequent phase. A second example is his unit on guessing or guesswork: the notion of teaching children how to guess, of legitimizing guessing, is clearly related to some of the ideas already expounded in Chapter 1. I remember Dan Fader making great play in his talks of the unacceptability of this immoral 'short-cut', as it was normally perceived by teachers. Looking back to one's own school days, it is not hard to imagine the censure one would have incurred if, in answer to the question, 'How did you work that out?' one had simply and smilingly replied, 'I guessed, sir!'

De Bono's advocacy of training in thinking, although perhaps vulnerable to misapplication, seems cogent, particularly in the light of my arguments in favour of structures:[5]

> We cannot rely on skills developed in the natural course of events unless the natural course of events has been especially rich in a variety of situations both narrow and broad. As with the typist, it might be better to make some deliberate effort to train skills directly.

After remarking on children's normal tendency to argue through force of personality rather than of argument, he lists some effects of instruction and practice in thinking as observed by teachers:

1 More listening to other people and less talking across people
2 Less egocentricity
3 Thinking used as exploration instead of just to support or defend a particular point of view
4 Less giggling or whispering
5 Less abuse and shouting down and more tolerance of other views
6 Use of thinking modes other than the purely critical
7 Knowing what to do instead of just waiting for an idea to arrive
8 Less wandering off into irrelevancy
9 More willingness to think about new subjects instead of dismissing them as ridiculous or irrelevant
10 More confidence.

These remarks apply especially to thinking or discussing in groups. The changes arise as much from practice in the group situation and in the opportunity for 'thinking' as from the actual structure of the lessons. Nevertheless a change in skill has been observed.

Apart from the strategies suggested by de Bono, others merit exploration, for example the whole idea of the use and imitation of models. Some possibilities may already have been suggested by the 'patently obvious' game where the availability of a register that is readily imitated definitely aids fluency. The general point about imitation is that if properly handled it can make new structures available and, *through them*, different ways of thinking: 'proper handling' will mean a primary emphasis on playful, exploratory activity though an element of analysis may be needed in order to make play fruitful. If I can take an example from my own work, having recently seen Alan Bennett's television series, *Talking Heads*, I have begun to explore with students some of the monologue techniques which Bennett exploits so brilliantly.[6]

One could prolong the list of possible structures and strategies indefinitely. Most of those claiming attention will, however, occur in subsequent chapters. Talking will penetrate, inform and interact with virtually every activity in English. As we will see this is particularly necessary when we consider writing, an activity that is very rarely associated with exploration, let alone with mental play. We need, however, to bear constantly in mind the fact that 'oral English' (hateful phrase – is the old-fashioned opposite 'anal English', one wonders?) must be the soil out of which everything else grows.

Notes

1 Tolstoy, 'On teaching the rudiments', a pedagogical article from *Yasnaya Polyana* in (1972) *Tolstoy on Education*, trans. by Leo Weiner, Chicago, Ill: University of Chicago Press, p. 47.

2 This challenged real experts to identify *weird* objects, often patented.
3 A. Cullum (1971) *The Geranium on the Window Sill Just Died but Teacher You Went Right On*, New York: Harlin Quist.
4 See for example Edward de Bono (1983) *Teachers' Notes (1) for CORT Thinking Materials*, published for the Cognitive Research Trust by Pergamon Press, pp. 21 and 42. See also Edward de Bono (1976) *Teaching Thinking*, London: Temple Smith, p. 46.
5 Edward de Bono (1983) op. cit., pp. 41 and 47.
6 Alan Bennett (1988) *Talking Heads*, London: BBC Publications.

3 Thinking and writing

Problems: hindrances to thinking in writing

And so each venture
Is a new beginning, a raid on the inarticulate.

(T. S. Eliot, 'East Coker (v)' from Four Quartets)

That process of raid, or persuasion, or ambush, or dogged hunting, or surrender, is the kind of thinking we have to learn and if we do not somehow learn it, then our minds lie in us like the fish in the pond of a man who cannot fish.

(Hughes 1967: 57)

Do children like composition? Do children ever ask to be allowed to write as they ask to be allowed to draw? Do their faces brighten when you say, 'We are all going to write a composition this afternoon'?

(Sampson 1921: 85)

I remember sitting alone in the worn urban classroom where my students had just written their first essays and where I now began to read them, hoping to be able to assess quickly the sort of task that lay ahead of us that semester. But the writing was so stunningly unskilled that I could not begin to define the task nor even sort out the difficulties. I could only sit there, reading and re-reading the alien papers, wondering what had gone wrong and trying to understand what I at this eleventh hour of my students' academic lives could do about it.[1]

The Excuse

Teresa
dark scared Teresa
has just confessed
she mainlines heroin

she has raised bail
for her numerous
step fathers and brothers
several times

she has slept
with more machos
than she can remember

she has worked in canneries and fields
since she was seven

her phantasies
linked to the spoon
match and needle
include tennis courts
picnics with lovers
pots of azaleas
swimming pools
a penthouse
pastel appliances
white bedrooms
and babies

she just wanted me to know
why she couldn't do a paper
(Alice F. Worsley)[2]

However one views it, writing is neither natural nor easy: there is T. S. Eliot's 'intolerable wrestle with words and their meanings' to contend with; there is the problem of the difference in speed of thought and of hand – early writers cope with the problems of transcription and of thinking at the same time; and then there is their growing awareness of conventions that should be observed.

As the years of schooling go by writing may become easier for some children; for only a very few can it be said to become natural. The first and possibly overriding reason for this is that teachers' efforts combine to emphasize its difficulty and in so doing divorce it from properly reflective processes, let alone play and experiment. There is, after all, such a lot that 'needs to be taught', such a lot that may in consequence become to the child an oppressive set of obligations; just as writing may easily become 'composition' – not too far removed in its style and impact from that described by George Sampson some seventy years ago.

For some years now I have run with my students a week's residential course on 'Techniques and Resources for Personal Writing', which seeks to explore the connections between speaking, writing and drama in as many ways as possible. The participants are about fifty 12–13-year-old children chosen from schools all over Somerset as being particularly able or showing special promise in English. The pupils are split into four subgroups, each looked after by three or four PGCE students who also supervise their open-air activities in the afternoons. In addition, each student has special responsibility for three or four pupils from the subgroup; the intention here is to provide opportunity for individual counselling, rather on the lines suggested by Donald Graves (1983). Since the working day runs from 9 am till 9.30 pm there are plenty of opportunities, some of the most fruitful of these being outside 'formal' sessions – perhaps even during 'dormitory duty'.

At the end of their week, in a final lead-session three years ago, the children answered a questionnaire about aspects of the writing process, their own development and experience as learners, being also encouraged to mention any English teaching practices which they had found irritating in the past. The questions were not, however, laid out on a form, but asked and explained by me as being matters that we really wanted to know more about. Their responses were nearly all serious attempts to *help us*.

In the rest of the book evidence from this source will for simplicity be referred to as 'Kilve', from the name of the centre where the courses are held. Obviously the sample used is small and highly unrepresentative but given the basic normality of these children their views are often just articulate expressions of feelings shared by less gifted peers. In any case their views are not adduced to *prove* anything but rather to give children's authentic voices a chance to be heard.[3]

When asked to give account of their development – their autobiographies as writers – they described very clearly the obligations referred to earlier; some of these were all the more strongly felt precisely because they were 'gifted', the highly motivated offspring of highly motivated parents. Anticipating this, our work over the years has often concentrated on trying to loosen them up because, as victims of their own school success record, they find new things risky and in particular they *have to be taught to play*.

> When I first started writing stories they were really stupid, I don't think I enjoyed writing much at first.

> When I went to school first I liked reading and writing, but because of my handwriting my teacher didn't. I wrote at home and read an awful lot when I got to F School. I didn't read very much and I stopped writing as much. I fell in with bad company, gradually I began to pull out and I started reading again and I began to write with a few quite good poems. I wrote one and read it to the school and they didn't believe I wrote it.

> When I was a baby my writing was boring. I used no big words and spelling was bad. My mum was the first person to place a pencil in my hand and she taught me to write. Over the years my punctuation has improved a great deal, my words have grown and my handwriting is far better than it used to be. Now that I can understand better I write better. The more information goes in the better writing comes out. My teacher also helps by making me use correct language not slang or swearing.

It is surprising to find that a fair proportion of these 'gifted' show not merely a sense of obligation to get it (in teacher's terms) 'right' but also an obvious anxiety and a tendency towards self-deprecation. Fortunately however, there are others who express a sense of comfort and achievement – even the kind of delight expressed in the next writer's first line:

When I first started writing I thought that I had found a new invention. I remember writing a twenty-one page story in infant school about Chicken Licken. It took me weeks and when I had finished I thought it was the best work I'd ever done. In primary school I did not do enough writing during the day so I started writing stories at home. Now I feel that writing helps me in a lot of subjects. I really enjoy writing because I find it relaxing.

A similar zest runs through the next account, but the reader should note just how early the notion of form and structure in writing was suggested to this lad.

I started off writing at about two. I only wrote scribbles then. The person who first taught me to write was my mum. As I progressed to infants the scribbling became more story like. However a story could be 'One day a boy went for a walk in the woods and he met a tiger but he killed the tiger and ran home and lived happily ever after.' I can remember being told by my last teachers of infants school:

'A story must have a beginning, a middle and an end.'

At around my first year at junior school I wrote my master piece 'Captain Morgan'. That story was about 12 sides of exercise paper long. My stories got longer and better. I had a tendency to write impossible explanations which no one except I could work out. In the first year at comprehensive I wrote 'Escape from St. Helena'. A story part fact and fiction with a fictional escape of Napoleon from his island prison of St. Helena. I also wrote Escape from a fantasy adventure story. My best story so far has been 'Ach tis vinegar' another fantasy adventure story.

For George Sampson (1921), drawing was associated in children's minds with pleasure, with playful exploration. Composition on the other hand was 'a wasteful and useless activity' associated both with inappropriate tasks – 'Tom Brown pretending to be Sir Thomas Browne' and compelled to write on topics like 'A loaf of bread' or 'Unpunctuality is the Mother of Invention' – and inappropriate procedures, for example the absurdity of demanding 'that all boys in a class must be writing on the same subject at the same time'.

'I shall doubtless be told,' Sampson says, later in Chapter 3 of *English for the English* (1921), 'that nowadays we do not expect our children to write essays and that the whole subject of composition has undergone a revolution. I can only reply. "Plus ça change, plus c'est la même chose"'. Nearly seventy years on there remain some of the same impediments. When the fifty children at Kilve were asked what kinds of writing of English they least enjoyed, there was a variety of responses – from book reviews to fairy stories – but a common feature of disliked writing tasks was that they were *imposed.* This notion was implicit in nearly every task quoted and often explicit. For the record, the most disliked writing tasks – with number of hostile votes shown in parentheses were – Poetry (14), Poetry with rhyme (8), Writing descriptions (7), Writing on set themes (5), Writing on set storylines (3), Writing (long) stories (5), and, yes, *Writing essays* (5)!

In answer to a later question – '*Are there any things that have irritated you in school with specific reference to reading and writing in English, behaviour of teachers etc.?'* – the theme of 'imposition' was again prominent, for example:

> Having to write Essays and stories on boring topics all through the year, with a very boring teacher who waffled on and on. Writing poems when you've got a good idea in your head.

> When the teachers tell you the title of a project and you have to stick to it. Our teacher never asks if you want to write on that subject. You just have to do it.

> Things at school which have irritated me are when we had a teacher who would not let us work in a choice of ways, but set it all for us and wouldn't take any notice of our views.

> When we are given essays with really boring and stupid titles. Writing out the same poem or story hundreds of times to stick on walls, put in best, etc. We have to write about school library books we read, and do a review on them when I never read them, I read my own books and just put down that the books were boring so I have tried another one.

As the last writer indicates, there are ways by which a bright pupil can defeat the system, but one is struck by the recurrence of the word 'essay'. Last year I followed this up and asked the course how many were used to the word being employed by teachers in the last year of junior school and/or the first year of secondary: thirty-three out of forty-eight hands went up immediately. Perhaps Sampson is still right.

Where the emphasis remains deeply rooted in old concepts children learn above all *not* to use writing in various personal, reflective, exploratory or playful ways. Where neatness is paramount, crossing out becomes a sin and thinking goes out of the window. Less able pupils learn also that writing is difficult; that they are not much good at it; that evaluation is the teacher's mystical prerogative. Like much abler children – including many at Kilve each year – all their learning points to the fact that writing has not much to do with their own thoughts but a great deal to do with arranging words. The net result is seen in 'compositions', such as the following example on the O level exam topic. Admittedly this goes back to 1965 but topics have changed rather more rapidly than styles.

The appeal which an area of natural beauty has for me
(Written by a girl in the second stream of a girls' high school)

I think the countryside is truly magnificent. It allows one to escape from the everyday bustle of the city life and to enter into a beautiful garden of tranquility.

    I can think of nothing better to set off in the car on a bright summer day and venture forth into the splendour of the quaint little villages which are a symbol of Britain's beauty spots. The tiny grey-bricked houses, with their red-tiled roofs are gaily decorated with flowers and Garlands around the porchs. In front of the little door there is probably a stream, and the cool, calm water dances merrily over the pebbles and it winds its way through the fields and towns until it can no longer be seen and it joins up with the sea. Some of the cottages have thatched roofs and the walls are pure white in colour. There are little window boxes full of plants and the whole appearance of the cottage is most exotic. It is no wonder that the tourists consider England as a most gorgeous and wonderful country.

In the Lake District one is able to see the charm of the natural countryside displayed in the effectiveness that the trees and hedges have, surrounding the delicately shaded blue of the water. Around the lakes are woodlands and orchards full of delicious fruits that are so tempting to pick. The narrow lanes of the country wind their way in and out of the villages like the shuttle weaves in and out of the loom. Some of these roads are like a tree arched avenue, where the trees bend over and join in the middle.

When I visit these delightful places of interest I like to see the old traditions which are still taking place today. I remember particularly while on an outing in the very beautiful Yorkshire Dales I saw a village wedding the couple arrived at the old church in a coach led by two dapple-grey ponies. The church bells were sounding melodiously and everywhere there was rejoicing. We then climbed our way up the dusty covered tracks across the moors and woodland and I may mention that it was a very difficult journey in the car, and quite a number of times we had to clamber out and push it over some bog that had bedded down the wheels.

My most thrilling experience in the countryside was when we stopped for a night to sleep out in the open. It was very exciting, we made camp near the river and all through the silence of the night we could hear the gentle ripples of the waves. The moon was out and it cast a light over the trees and it gave them the appearance of bent old hags leaning over. Old Mr. Owl was wide awake and was perched in a tree, hooting away all the night. I was extremely glad to be covered up and to be snuggled up tight in my sleeping bag.

The next day we continued our journey through the sleepiness of the towns and villages and we arrived at a wood where a village fete was being held. All the village folk were there and all the jolly farmers, which wore their old trousers and big wellington boots and not forgetting the stick they carry and the old faithful sheep dog, which walked continuously by their side. The village activities are quite different from the city because everyone knows each other and make their fellow neighbours well and truly welcomed.

To be in the country among natural beauty is the ideal thing for me. I love to smell the grass and the wild flowers growing in the hedges. To see the Combine Harvesters doing their share of providing the corn, wheat and barley for the big industrial towns. Gone are the days when you could see the farmers wife busy serving country teas in the fields but it is still nice to ponder about these wonderful things. At least the rest of the countrysides natural beauty is preserved and I sincerely hope it will be for a long time to come.

Out of her class of thirty I recall that twenty-nine wrote on the same topic. Every essay began with a plan crossed out with parallel, diagonal, ruler-drawn lines and marked off by two parallel, horizontal, ruler-drawn lines. They had been thoroughly 'taught'. In Ted Hughes's terms, they had in the process become 'false to themselves':

All falsities in writing – and the consequent dry rot that spreads into the whole fabric – come from the notion that there is a stylistic ideal which exists in the abstract, like a special language, to which all men might attain. But teachers of written English should have nothing to do with that, which belongs rather to the study of manners and group jargon. Their words should not be 'How to write' but 'How to try to say what you really mean' – which is part of the search for self-knowledge and perhaps, in one form or another, grace.

(Hughes 1967: 12)

Or, as D. J. Enright put it in his poem, 'Blue Umbrellas':[4]

Oh our mistaken teachers! –
It was not a proper regard for words that we need.
But a decent regard for things, those older creatures
and more real.

The spiritual dimension: kinds of writing and kinds of thinking

Before we can usefully think about strategies for encouraging writing, we need to be clear about the preconditions. These have much to do with what I have called classroom climate but even that is dependent on two sets of other considerations: the spiritual and the theoretical.

The spiritual preconditions have to do with the way that teachers view the lives of children, or human life in general; with what teachers conceive their role to be; with their beliefs or faith. Something of this dimension – which is elusive and prone to facile misrepresentations – comes through in Buber's words, toughly, clearly and unsoggily; especially when he is seeking to illuminate the relationship of teacher and taught. The word 'empathy', now often trivialized in commercial training manuals for salespersons and reduced to a series of sympathetic tricks to seduce gullible customers, here regains the proper muscularity it had when Keats used it.

If education means to let a selection of the world affect a person through the medium of another person, then the one through whom this takes place, rather, who makes it take place through himself, is caught in a strange paradox. What is otherwise found only as grace, inlaid in the folds of life – the influencing of the lives of others with one's own life – becomes here a function and a law. But since the educator has to such an extent replaced the master, the danger has arisen that the new phenomenon, the will to educate, may degenerate into arbitrariness, and that the educator may carry out his selection and his influence from himself and his idea of the pupil, not from the pupil's own reality.

(Buber 1947: 127)

It is another example of the teacher's desire to teach distracting his proper attention from the reality of the child. As Buber goes on:

One only needs to read, say, the accounts of Pestalozzi's teaching method to see how easily, even with the noblest teachers, arbitrary self-will is mixed up with will. This is almost always due to an interruption or a temporary flagging of the act of inclusion, which is not merely regulative for the realm of education, as for other realms, but is actually constitutive; so that the realm of education acquires its true and proper force from the constant return of this act and the constantly renewed connexion with it. The man whose calling it is to influence the being of persons that can be determined, must experience this action of his (however much it may have assumed the form of non-action) ever anew from the other side.

(Buber 1947: 127)

We come now to the core of the argument: the need for teachers to hear themselves, to stand outside themselves in order to attend properly to those in their care:

> Without the action of his spirit being in any way weakened he must at the same time be over there, on the surface of that other spirit which is being acted upon – and not of some conceptual, contrived spirit, but all the time the wholly concrete spirit of this individual and unique being who is living and confronting him, and who stands with him in the common situation of 'educating' and 'being educated' (which is indeed one situation, only the other is at the other end of it). It is not enough for him to imagine the child's individuality, nor to experience him directly as a spiritual person and then to acknowledge him. Only when he catches himself 'from over there', and feels how it affects one, how it affects this other human being, does he recognize the real limit, baptize his self will in Reality and make it true will, and renew his paradoxical legitimacy. He is of all men the one for whom inclusion may and should change from an alarming and edifying event into an atmosphere.
>
> But however intense the mutuality of giving and taking with which he is bound to his pupil, inclusion cannot be mutual in this case. He experiences the pupil's being educated, but the pupil cannot experience the educating of the educator. The educator stands at both ends of the common situation, the pupil only at one end.

(Buber 1947: 127–8)

Buber is trying to convey in general terms the teacher's stance. Marjorie Hourd is interested in the same thing but with particular reference to the interface between the insights of literature and those of psychoanalysis – especially as these affect the thinking and feeling processes reflected in children's writing.

> The truth is that we have to learn to live with our poetic natures. This is no sentimental notion, but one which demands a particular kind of alertness – not the 'pay attention', 'listen to me', 'don't turn around' kind of attention, but one that requires the use of what has been called 'the third ear', which listens as much to what is not being said as to what is, to the half-regained, the not yet achieved – and for this mode of attention, it is asserted by poets and psychologists alike, we need to cultivate a state of reverie. Keats accepted reverie as a means of 'strengthening the intellect'. His advice was 'to make up one's mind about nothing' and to let it be 'a thoroughfare for all thoughts – not a select party'. Freud, through his early experience and especially with the French neurologist Charcot, was attracted to just such a passive-active approach to the patient which he developed into the technique of

free-association. Charcot once remarked to Freud: 'You must look at the same things over and over again until they speak to you.'[5]

Once again it is necessary to emphasize the unsentimentality of such a viewpoint. This comes out in her comments on certain early experiments with 'Free-Writing' in which lessons partly learnt from the use of association techniques in psychiatry were too enthusiastically reapplied. In its acuteness, empathy and humour, Miss Hourd's view of both children and the classroom never lost touch with reality:

> Thinking for oneself is hard work and often brings pain to the mind. It must not be confused with that loose and uncommitted way of thinking which is a form of thoughtlessness. Free writing can easily be abused. There is no reason why teachers should condone everything that comes from a child's pen. And one must watch for those children who try to be free, in order to please teacher or fall in with a fashion. And children must watch out for teachers who are only ready for what they expect.[6]

The theoretical dimension, and what it means in practice

Whether or not the particular passages cited above convince the reader of the need for a spiritual dimension in any central core of belief, such a dimension is essential and is often best illuminated by writers whose concerns are wider than merely pedagogic ones. The spiritual may then be related to the theoretical dimension, to old and new knowledge about children's writing and ways of fostering it. The general position from which to discuss the development of facilitating conditions and strategies for writing is put very clearly by Susan Hackman (1987). She is writing to argue the case for writing in response to literature but her remarks on 'Thinking in Writing' have a much wider relevance:

> Encouraging pupils to write informally about their first responses to texts, and asking them to refine these responses in their own way, puts some of the emphasis back onto the reader and the reading, and away from received opinions and the artifice of examination discourse. It takes some of the pressure off the pupil to 'perform'. Personal engagement and reflection are encouraged.
>   . . . we write to find out if we have anything worth saying. We can write for ourselves, for our own purposes. It may be to our purpose to chisel away at a point until it comes clear, or just to generate raw ideas, or to chew over a problem or to get something straight in the mind. It may be simply to get into a stream of thought, or to see what a tentative idea comes out like. We often find out what we have to say only once we have started to say it.
>
> (Hackman 1987: 10)

To offer opportunities for such exploration in writing is a crucial step towards helping children to value their own minds in the way emphasized in Chapter 1. This function of writing is clearly recognized in the Cox Report (1989: para. 17.4): 'For the individual author, writing can have cognitive functions in clarifying and supporting thought.' Susan Hackman goes on to relate this process to the way 'real' writers operate:

> Writing teaches partly because it defines ideas more clearly but also because it generates new ones. We write ourselves into a subject. The reading self prompts the writing self with second thoughts and new ideas. Notice how a writer gropes after the next phrase by reading back over the preceding sentences. It is a way of cueing into the next idea. We also re-read to identify false notes, inaccuracies, errors of logic and inconsistencies. We act as a second person, interrogating what is written, arguing back or nodding approval. A productive inner dialogue is set up between ourselves as writers and ourselves as readers. This is what is meant by writing being a reflexive medium which is self-generating. It works on us as we work on it. . . .
>
> Writing is not a tool for thought in the sense that it tinkers with the thinking machinery like a spanner, nor is it a skill we are refining for the more efficient transmission of learning. It is learning. The reading experience of the pupil is framed in the words she writes; the words are the manifestation of her thinking, holding it in a form. Writing is unique in its qualities of explicitness, durability, privacy and versatility, but the best thing about it is that the process of writing is the process of thinking, forming ideas and learning.[7]

Given the dimensions already glanced at, we need both faith and knowledge if we are radically to alter children's perception of writing, to extend its range and to make it a vehicle for ways of thinking, feeling and perceiving. Donald Graves begins his credo on an optimistic note:

> Children want to write. They want to write the first day they attend school. This is no accident. Before they went to school they marked up walls, pavements, newspapers with crayons, chalk, pens or pencils . . . anything that makes a mark. The child's marks say, 'I am.'
>
> (Graves 1983: 3)

It is this conviction, perhaps more than anything else, which has made his work so influential; the faith in the child as learner, question-asker and answer-finder is more important than particular features of his 'method' apart from his notion of individual 'conferences' with child writers – to which aspect I shall return.

Writers on education are subject to fashion – they have their brief hour, feted by Her Majesty's Inspectorate or local authority – and then give way to the latest prophet. Fortunately truth – about children and writing in this case – does not suffer from built-in obsolescence. Given people's forgetfulness, however, it needs to be constantly rediscovered and practice to be reinterpreted in the light of new knowledge.

Thus we might not agree with George Sampson's (1921) specific proposals for gradually disciplining the pupil's writing, but in general his insights, intuitions, humour and common sense remain to refresh and invigorate us.

> The younger children should be encouraged to write and to write copiously. . . .
> Writing, as a regular exercise, should never be forced upon lower standard children.

The notion that what they write is to be looked at censoriously and discussed disagreeably should never enter their little heads. The assumption must be that it is splendid and that teacher will love to read it. The teacher who can get little boys and girls to pour themselves out freely on paper may be well satisfied.

(Sampson 1921: 81)

The assumption that 'teacher will love it' is crucial: as I have argued, teachers are not there just to be nice to or even love children, but to engender confidence through their patent interest and delight in the child's mind. The section of the Cox Report (1989: paras 17.67–17.71) which deals with the assessment of written work has a good deal to say about fostering 'a child's confidence in the exploration of ideas and the manner of their presentation' and about the way teachers should promote their growth. Way back in 1921 Sampson knew this too:

The boy would accept instruction on sentences [he argued] without the theological support of grammar. If there is one thing more pleasing and wholesome than anything else in the human boy, it is his entire disregard of first principles and his refusal to behave (in bulk) like the hypothetical child of educational treatises. That is what troubles young teachers: they have been led to expect the child, and they encounter children.

(Sampson 1921: 81)

Sampson's delight in children is echoed in Graves:

We lose out on the surprises children have for us because we don't let them write. Surprises come when children begin to control writing as a craft. Children learn to control writing because their teachers practise teaching as a craft. Both teachers and children see the control of the craft as a long, painstaking process with energy supplied along the way through the joy of discovery. Eight-year-old Amy surprised her teacher with this lead to her draft: 'A cheetah would make a sports car look like a turtle.'

(Graves 1983: 3)

To which Sampson might add: the problem is that teachers are not conditioned to enjoy being surprised.

The reader will recall the recurrent complaint from the children already quoted about imposition, about the lack of choice. Choice is something we rarely give pupils a chance to handle. Yet even a moderately motivated child may have quite a number of ideas and may spend time wrestling with the question 'How to begin?' Too many pupils who have sat chewing their pencils over this will testify to the paucity of help received, e.g. 'Stop worrying, James, and get on with it.' This possibly accompanied by the rider 'You've only got fourteen minutes!' But 'worrying', productively used, is thinking. And any real writer will tell you that getting started is very hard, and very important.

Mina Shaughnessy, in the passage quoted at the head of this chapter, was thinking about the predicament of children who had experienced years of failure and were now to undergo remediation in what was called the 'Basic Writing

Program'. Graves, starting from the other end as it were, tries to nip the problem in the bud through regular personal dialogue with the individual child: 'conferences'. The significance of this idea of dialogue is underlined by the complaints of the children at Kilve about lack of guidance, and about the inscrutability of the teachers' evaluation and reception of their work, for example:

> I did a really nice neat poem that was the result of everything my teacher had told me to do and I got C− for it!

> Last year, my English teacher, Mrs P, marked some pieces of work and gave me 17/20, 16/20, marks like that. The thing is she didn't write where I had gone wrong, so I couldn't correct myself and do it right next time.

> I was irritated in English (or was it?) by the lack of proper guidance. An SRA set cannot tell you half of the things that teachers should. The only proper English that teachers taught me were spellings.

> I was really irritated once in English when I'd put a great deal of effort into this story and my teacher didn't even bother to read it but put a great big red cross through all 6 pages (sides) because it was messy and he could see two spelling mistakes in the first line. As it turned out my writing wasn't the worst in the class anyway and those two spelling mistakes were the only ones in the whole story. I also get irritated when I'm set a story to write in say – by the end of the lesson and it's one I'll have to think about so I know I won't get it finished unless I hurry and then it's rubbish.

Graves's basic principles of 'conferencing' are outlined in the important chapter called 'Help the children speak first' (Graves 1983: 97–105). This deals with 'the specifics of helping children to speak and to continue to speak once they've started'. Young children (6- and 7-year-olds) enjoy being questioned in this new way, though older children 'wait longer before trusting the teacher'. However, Graves argues,

> it isn't long before children learn that the teacher does want to know what they know. The pauses mean something, that the teacher is giving time to the writer to speak.

His suggestions are notably practical. He begins with advice on sitting close to (rather than opposite) the child, and on the same level so that they can look at a piece of writing together. The important thing is for teachers to show themselves by the physical setting, to be 'advocate' rather than 'adversary'. Second, the teacher is advised to establish the comfort of a predictable routine so that the children know what is expected of them, that they are the ones who will speak first about how their writing is getting on. In this children learn also that the content, rather than the formal aspects of their writing, is the focus of the teaching interest.

The establishment of this routine enables the teacher to be subsequently more challenging but only after the initial barriers are broken down. The child may now be 'stretched' by the teacher because the teacher has first listened, then has asked questions relevant to [the child's] intention for writing in the first place.

No part of the 'Graves method' seems to be more important than his emphasis on the teacher's patience, a patience which is based on the conviction that the child really has something to say, and that the teacher can learn from it. The trick – as Marjorie Hourd had argued forty years earlier – is to

> Ask and Wait.
> Be prepared to get used to silence. Can you ask a question and wait fifteen seconds? Most children have a maximum of three to five seconds to respond to teacher queries. Fifteen seconds is a luxury for the child. In our research data I have video recordings of children who have waited forty-five seconds to respond to a question. The silence after the question is painful for me, the adult viewer. But the child knows the silence means it is his time to formulate a response . . . and he does. The child who had forty-five seconds to formulate an answer didn't acquire this ability overnight. Both he and his teacher gradually learned to use silence, starting at a ten- to fifteen-second wait.
> Children will use silence when the conference is predictable, when the setting is right, and when they believe you think they have something worthwhile to say. Just wait for it.
>
> (Graves 1983: 100)

All this is quite hard work as Graves admits:

> Listening to children is more a deliberate act than a natural one. It isn't easy to put aside personal preferences, anxieties about helping more children, or the glaring, mechanical errors that stare from the page. I mumble to myself, 'shut up, listen, and learn!'
>
> (Graves 1983: 100)

Two notes of reservation seem appropriate at this point, however. The first concerns the difficulty of translating the method into the secondary classroom, where the teachers are not in contact with the children for more than a few hours each week. Despite this, anyone who is won over by Graves's line of argument may be able to move *in the same direction*. (Herbert Kohl once suggested that one might move towards his concept of the 'open classroom' by having the classroom 'open' for a few minutes each day.) Though for the secondary teacher weekly conferences are not feasible, it may be possible, utilizing times when for example either project work or silent reading is in progress, to aim at monthly dialogues of this kind. Applied with conviction, this, almost on its own, could change the whole writing climate of the classroom, to say nothing of the pupils' view of 'marking'.

The second reservation concerns the kinds of writing to be attempted. In certain of these, as for example the situation evoked in Heaney's poem 'Playway' (quoted in Chapter 1) the teacher is promoting a certain kind of absorption. The pressure thus built up is a legitimate one and will be dissipated by discussion. As the poet said, 'If you talk about your idea for a poem, you'll probably lose the poem'. I shall return to this kind of 'absorption strategy' at the end of this chapter.

Contexts and strategies for writing

In order to break new ground, the teacher's main aim may be to create new contexts for writing.[8] An early slogan of the Writing Research Unit at the London University Institute of Education, 'Situations not kinds of writing', emphasized helping children to see what language was required by the demands of a particular situation; as opposed to the more familiar handing down of stylistic recipes. A second emphasis of the London team was on the search for new audiences to be written for – instead of the teacher (evaluator), examiner, or God. It may also be helpful to encourage children, as James Britton (1970) has suggested, to see a kind of triangular relationship in which they have to bear in mind *themselves* (and their purposes), their *subject*, and their *audience*.

Conditions for writing should be varied, in the interests of expanding experience and repertoire; they will also vary according to the way the teacher seeks to exploit his own strengths. The children from Kilve, most of whom came from at least relatively favoured backgrounds, tended to see writing as essentially a quiet and private activity. In answer to the question 'When and where do you write best?', twenty-five explicitly mentioned quietness; eleven explicitly mentioned solitude; nine mentioned settings which implied solitude; twenty-four explicitly associated these with home – with kitchens, living-rooms and bedrooms being particular places where they could find the comfort and relaxation they felt necessary. Sundays and evenings were preferred times.

I do not think this should be taken to prove that writing in class is inappropriate but rather to suggest that many classrooms, as they described them, had *none* of the desired characteristics, especially quiet. There was one classroom, for instance, under Miss B, who 'would have difficulty controlling a crippled mouse. Total chaos breaks out and those who want to work can't'. Another complained of 'People not concentrating on reading or writing. The teacher should try to keep silly people under control'. Control – for these perhaps unnaturally earnest youngsters – was a major source of concern. But there were other kinds of incompetence.

> In our class Mr G never explains things. He just uses the book. Also we never have to write essays about things we imagine. We never get taken to see things to describe it. Most of the lesson we just read a book. If we come to a word we don't understand he doesn't explain it to us. Also he doesn't like it when someone brings up a good poem. He changes it and then it isn't the same.

or

> Last year's English teacher was awful; she never thought the lesson out. We'd arrive and she'd say 'Oh, sit down and read, we'll do something else later'. Then she'd sit

day-dreaming and fiddling with her jewellery and we never did anything else. This
went on for most of the term.

Conditions like these only prove that badly run classrooms are as inimical to real
thinking as to real writing. Some of the more fortunate – about a dozen – *preferred*
writing in class and four mentioned that they liked being put under some
pressure. Another four who liked working at home in solitude also liked writing in
class '*when everyone else was writing*'.

In *Wishes, Lies, and Dreams* (1970: 27–9) Kenneth Koch gives a refreshing
account of both his teaching and learning as what we might now call a 'poet in
residence', over several months in an American primary school. One of his
discoveries bears particularly on the question discussed above.

> A surprising discovery I made at this school was that children enjoyed writing poems
> at school more than at home. I had assumed that like grownup writers they would
> prefer to be comfortable, quiet, and alone when they wrote, but I was wrong. Once it
> had to be done away from school, poetry was part of the detestable category
> 'homework', which cuts one off from the true pleasures of life; whereas in school it
> was a welcome relief from math, spelling, and other required subjects. Closing their
> heavy books to hear about a new idea for a poem made the children happy and
> buoyant. There was also the fact of their all being there in the room, writing together.
> No time for self-consciousness or self-doubts; there was too much activity: everyone
> was writing and talking and jumping around. And it was competitive in a mild and
> exhilarating way: it was what everyone was doing and everyone could do it.

In this particular setting, with quite young children, there was a good deal of noise
and infectious excitement. Neither of these features need be permanently absent
from secondary classrooms but the conditions and contexts for writing will need
to vary. In Koch's work the emphasis is very much on experimentation, often
working from set (supportive) formulae. For example there is 'I used to be . . . but
now . . .' where the task is to complete this 'couplet' in perhaps ten different ways
– an exercise enjoyed by children at secondary school too. Other exercises are
focused more on pure verbal (even nonsense) play. In all, the children are being
taught in Michael Oakshott's memorable phrase to 'savour the delight of
utterance' (quoted in Britton 1970: 61).

Even at that level play may have the important element of challenge. I referred
in Chapter 2 to a certain calculated arbitrariness as contributing to this and one of
the most interesting and daring applications of the principle was designed by
Robin Chambers. Members of his class were asked to fill in four numbered grids.
One of these dealt with characters, another with objects, another with situations,
another with settings. A child could then choose a random number, say 19, and
no. 19, on each grid, might yield some such combination as the following: an
elderly scientist, a blasted heath, a quarrel, and a stick of rock. These were the
elements that child then had to weave together in a story – a combination mad

enough to intrigue many who prided themselves on their consistent indifference.[9]

Another rich and under-used field for experiment is both parody and imitation of suitable models. One of the advantages here is that it can bring analytical and creative thinking into playful collaboration. To take a single example: just before the last Kilve course I had been much preoccupied with house-hunting. Having issued them with sets of unwanted estate-agents' particulars, I gave factual details of a particularly unappealing residence and invited them to describe it in estate-agentese. They did it well and zestfully. Frameworks of all kinds may be useful in liberating new ways of thinking and writing at the same time as extending linguistic repertoire. This point is also emphasized in the Cox Report (1989: para. 7.20) – 'imitation of a writer's use of language involves an *active* response that requires the pupil to make meaning yet to show a grasp of the original author's craft at the same time'.

Some of the most interesting strategies have been devised to circumvent observed and recurrent difficulties experienced by young writers. Children with a long history of failure in writing may be materially helped, for example, by some of the ideas in Peter Elbow's intriguing *Writing Without Teachers* (1973). The foundation stone of this is regular 'freewriting' in which the aim is to encourage fluency and to get rid of the editor in your head. (The exercise is also salutary for English graduates.) There is discussion later, however, of editing, and of recognizing 'garbage'.

> The most effective way I know to improve your writing is to do freewriting exercises regularly. At least three times a week. They are sometimes called 'automatic writing', 'babbling', or 'jabbering' exercises. The idea is simply to write for ten minutes (later on, perhaps fifteen or twenty). Don't stop for anything. Go quickly without rushing. Never stop to look back, to cross something out, to wonder how to spell something, to wonder what word or thought to use, or to think about what you are doing. If you can't think of a word or a spelling, just use a squiggle or else write, 'I can't think of it'. Just put down something. The easiest thing is just to put down whatever is in your mind. If you get stuck it's fine to write 'I can't think what to say, I can't think what to say' as many times as you want; or repeat the last word you wrote over and over again; or anything else. The only requirement is that you never stop.
>
> (Elbow 1973: 3)

As the book progresses, the emphasis turns progressively towards the thinking processes involved. I quoted earlier from Susan Hackman, and her idea about 'productive inner dialogue' between self as writer and as reader is dealt with by Elbow in a section where the interaction is described by the metaphor *cooking*; he also lays special emphasis on contradictions and conflicts in the writer's thinking:

> Just as two people, if they let their ideas interact, can produce ideas or points of view that neither could singly have produced, a lone person, if he learns to maximize the

interaction among his own ideas or points of view, can produce new ones that didn't seem available to him.

(Elbow 1973: 50–1)

While Elbow is trying to circumvent some of the problems that result in the kinds of major 'blockage' and incompetence shown in the students Mina Shaughnessy felt initially defeated by, other strategies exist for coping with more limited problems. One of the most interesting of these concerns the vexed subject of what used to be called 'essay planning'. I have cast doubt earlier on the supposed pre-eminence of logical procedures. Injunctions to the hesitant wretch to 'think before he speaks' testify to the same pathetic delusion.

'How', asks Tony Buzan (1974: 66) 'does the brain which is speaking and the brain which is receiving the words, deal with them *internally*?' He goes on:

> The answer is that the brain is most certainly not dealing with them in simple lists and lines. You can verify this by thinking of the way in which your own thought processes work while you are speaking to someone else. You will observe that although a single line of words is coming out, a continuing and enormously complex process of sorting and selecting is taking place in your mind throughout the conversation. Whole networks of words and ideas are being juggled and interlinked in order to communicate a certain meaning to the listener.

If it is complicated when one is speaking, it is far worse when one is writing. In much of this book I am trying to bring together, into coherence, a set of ideas which I have felt strongly, had glimmerings of, feelings and intuitions gathered from many sources over a considerable period of time. When things do start to cohere that's *exciting*. And that makes certain kinds of planning even more impossible. I could and do try to write myself into the swing – a useful but painful process which normally entails automatically crossing out the first five pages. But this is not enough and certainly linear plans do not help, because when things are moving ideas come not as single spies but in battalions. What to put down first? How to put down twelve things at the same time? The only device that I have found really helpful in this predicament – to students as well as myself – is something like that suggested by Buzan (1974). In part of the chapter on 'Brain patterns for recall and creative thinking', he discusses 'The brain and advanced noting':

> If the brain is to relate to information most efficiently the information must be structured in such a way as to 'slot in' as easily as possible. It follows that if the brain works primarily with key concepts in an interlinked and integrated manner, our notes and our word relations should in many instances be structured in this way rather than in traditional 'lines'.
>
> Rather than starting from the top and working down in sentences or lists, one should start from the centre or main idea and branch out as dictated by the individual ideas and general form of the central theme.

(Buzan 1974: 87–8)

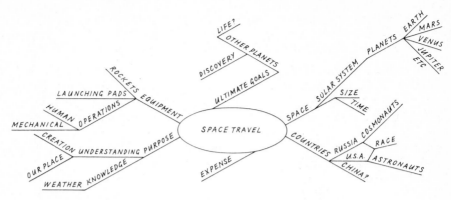

Figure 1 Initial ideas jotted around a centre
Source: Buzan 1974: 88

As Buzan argues, a pattern such as that outlined in Figure 1 has a number of advantages over the linear form of note-taking.

1 The centre or main idea is more clearly defined.
2 The relative importance of each idea is clearly indicated. More important ideas will be nearer the centre and less important ideas will be near the edge.
3 The links between the key concepts will be immediately recognizable because of their proximity and connection.
4 As a result of the above, recall and review will be both more effective and more rapid.
5 The nature of the structure allows for the easy addition of new information without messy scratching out or squeezing in, etc.
6 Each pattern made will look and be different from each other pattern. This will aid recall.
7 In the more creative areas of note making such as essay preparations etc., the open-ended nature of the pattern will enable the brain to make new connections far more readily.

(Buzan 1974: 89)

Buzan's ideas here form the basis for a new approach for writing of an extended discursive kind and as he goes on to show, they can be further developed. Working on the first diagram shown, I have encouraged students to look for ideas that are in some way related – perhaps using arrows or numbers to indicate such relationships. If there has been a considerable flood of initial ideas or – as often happens – if the search for relationships itself generates more ideas, there may be a need to break the diagram up into mini-constellations. At this stage we are working with ideas that are, in a sense, still *latent* – for two reasons: first, the initial ideas still exist merely as labels or headings; second, the kinds of relationship that are indicated by arrows are not yet properly articulated. The student has glimpsed a relationship but has not yet found words to express it.

The diagrammatic phases can now be reduced to a linear form, though those who get used to the system may find the numbering of items on the diagram sufficient for their purposes. For the less practised, however, it may be helpful

1 to list the items in a possible order, and then
2 to try, alongside each, in a sentence to express the gist of what they want to say.

To give an example, a diagram on 'Life in the country' might show the item 'transport'. What is not clear is whether this idea came into the student's head because transport is a problem in rural areas, because it is the subject of official neglect, because individuals have to be more self-reliant, or what. What the student is groping towards may be made clear if this idea has been linked with another. In which case the question is 'Why?' Explain the connection. I believe that the difference between a *heading* and what used to be called a *key sentence* is something that can still usefully be taught. Equally the use of diagrams may help to show up the fact that a little group of constellated ideas occurred because these were examples or illustrations of a main thesis not yet articulated.

The distinction between main idea and illustration used to be taught analytically through precis. I am more interested in its constructive use in helping the students to learn the rudiments of developing an argument and *through this* mere technical trick discovering yet again that they have something – indeed quite a lot – to say.

The great virtue of some such approach, as Buzan advocates, is that it is fast and can cope with a lot of ideas: because it offers what Witkin might call a 'holding form' without the interference caused by a premature inner demand for explicitness and order in what should be the crucial, thinking, stage of the operation. In other contexts, the same argument can be adduced in favour of various brainstorming techniques.

We may take description as a further area where teacher strategies need to be designed to circumvent problems known to be commonly experienced by learners. A surprising number of children at Kilve have admitted that they find this kind of writing difficult. Many of the problems involved are, however, susceptible to teaching as the suggestions of Ted Hughes, including those quoted at the end of this chapter, make clear. Moreover, the 'problem of description' may be broken down into more specific kinds of difficulties which may be circumvented by appropriate strategies: these may help the pupil to solve problems of organization, to explore possibilities without feeling pressured, to learn how to focus, how to select, how to emphasize, and so on.[10] Sometimes the difficulty is compounded by over-reliance on the use of what is called stimulus material. This reliance has been trenchantly criticized by Michael Benton[11] for its assumption that so long as the stimulus produces a response, appropriate learning has occurred. The learning may in fact have been of a quite different kind: in the hands of a mechanistic teacher, even less able children can learn to recognize a 'stimulus' when they see one, even if the teacher 'pretends' that it's actually a *poem*; and if they're anxious to please the pedagogue they can rapidly learn to appear stimulated. As we shall see in the next chapter, there is a place for the technique but attention has to be given to the way the ground is prepared for it. Stimuli go wrong most often when divorced from context and when no procedural help in 'responding' is offered. Purely Pavlovian (S-R) writing is as much an imposition as the old essay but responding to a stimulus may be very fruitful if it grows out of a conversation already set up, or from relevant reading. Imposition in this case consists not in pointing children's heads in a particular direction but in suggesting to them what they see or feel, or 'ought' to see and feel.

Occasionally however, a teacher may find an inspired way of circumventing known or foreseeable difficulty. Valerie Bartoletto, working with young primary school-children in British Columbia, saw straight description as too abstract for her charges. She had other difficulties – chiefly the unadventurousness of a class of well-disciplined, polite, middle-class children. Her 'hardest task was to inspire unconventional thinking; to give the children permission to be extraordinary'.[12]

Since description in school often consists in presenting a more or less inadequate verbal picture of something which the audience (in nearly all cases the teacher) is known to be already familiar with, the task does not encourage commitment or conviction. Valerie Bartoletto saw this clearly:

> Always I asked them to tell me something I didn't know, something that was true for them.[13]

As often happens the solution came gradually. First, from Koch's *Rose, Where Did You Get that Red?*[14] and from the children's enjoyment of Blake's 'Tyger', she derived the idea of being able to *speak directly* to an object or an animal. The full possibilities were clarified for her through her reading of the book by Albert Cullum (1971) from which I have already quoted (*The Geranium on the Window Sill Just Died but Teacher You Went Right On*).[15] In this, each poem is the words of a child directly addressed to a teacher.

I have argued earlier that suitable frameworks and models can make available new ways of thinking. This model seems to me to have enormous possibilities at various levels of age or sophistication but particularly for young children. Talking *at* or *to*, by virtue of its close connection with everyday ways of speaking and feeling, offers a real opportunity to break new ground and frees young children from the daunting need to make statements. Almost from the outset Valerie Bartoletto discovered

> Children write more freely when they talk to animals or pretend to be the animal than if they try to write *about* the animal.[16]

The model provided by Cullum's poems moved things a stage farther. Bartoletto discovered that many were reluctant to write about school in the same way but she found parallel opportunities:

I asked them to write their poems as if they were talking to the person who had offended them ... storekeepers, babysitters, siblings, doctors, piano-teachers, neighbours, parents etc.[17]

One or two bolder spirits adopted the Cullum model in content as well as form, however, for example:

Mrs Grescoe, why do I have to write a poem? I hate writing poems. You look at Debbies and you laugh. You look at mine and its just another bunch of words. So Mrs. Grescoe, tell me why do I have to write a poem?

(Lenore Frank)

This technique works at various levels. Though the work described above is in its primitive form, the stance of the writer – where he addresses an object or person about which he has strong feelings – is the same as that of many sophisticated writers, and of odes in particular. Of itself, this stance – by its freedom from the particular constraints of 'description' – actually makes it easier for the child initially to *attend* to the object or person in question and hence to articulate the thoughts and feelings which this attention evokes.

As the example of Valerie Bartoletto reminds us, the need is for the teacher to be constantly observing the performance and the difficulties of those in her charge: there has to be constant experiment with frameworks which might make possible new ways of thinking and new modes of utterance. A particular strength of Valerie's technique in this context was its closeness to natural modes of speech. The connection with speech has already been referred to when considering discussion and argument but there is hardly an aspect of English where it cannot be usefully exploited. With older children, for example, where attempts at written description may be more appropriate, it may be very helpful to relate this activity to what Rosen and Rosen (1973) in *The Language of Primary School Children* have called 'talking while observing'.

At a later stage one finds teachers who still believe that narrative and description are among the easier modes (i.e. suitable for the less able examination candidates). This may be the case if these tasks are kept in proper relation to oral activities; narrative, for example, might be rendered much less problematic were it to be built on extended experience of anecdote and oral story-telling. This is a rich field for exploration, as indeed is the wider subject of the conditions which help children to incubate ideas.

Ted Hughes's 'recipe' is pertinent here and also links interestingly with some features of the 'Bartoletto method' described above. In a note for teachers at the end of his chapter on 'Learning to Think' he writes

Without turning English lessons into Yoga sessions it ought to be possible to put the ideas in this chapter into practice fairly easily.

Practice in simple concentration on a small, simple object is the most valuable of all mental exercises. Any object will do. Five minutes at a time is long enough, and one minute is enough to begin with. If the exercise is repeated every lesson, the results will show.

The writing exercise follows from this. The pupil takes any small, simple object, and while concentrating on it gives it the treatment described in the Note to Chapter One: full-out descriptive writing, to a set length, in a set time, in a loose verse form.

The descriptions will be detailed, scientific in their objectivity and microscopic attentiveness. After some exercises of this sort, the pupil should be encouraged to extend the associations out from the object in every direction, as widely as possible, keeping the chosen object as the centre and anchor of all his statements.

Once the pupil has grasped the possible electrical connections between the objective reality and some words of his, this exercise, which at first sight seems dull enough, becomes absorbingly exciting. Even where it produces poor results, the efforts towards this kind of perception and description affects the way the pupil looks at, and attends to, everything.

Where this type of exercise can be pursued intensively, the same object should be tackled repeatedly, four or five times, on different days.

(Hughes 1967: 63–4)

Knowing teachers as well as children, Hughes is careful by his reference to yoga to allay anxieties. He was right to do so; James Moffett in a fairly recent visit to Australia undoubtedly raised some hackles by an evident penchant for the mystical. Yet when in one of his later books[18] he drew a comparison between some thinking techniques for writing and the first phase of medieval meditation procedures – 'the composition of place' (i.e. the sustained and serious effort of the mind to evoke the scene or setting associated with the action or theme to be meditated on) – I believe he was suggesting a really fruitful analogy.

Silence, whether compliant, bored or sullen, is something which schools appear still to value. Productive silence however is a condition which too few strive for. Hughes's suggestions for concentration, like the method advocated in *Sense and Sensitivity* (Creber 1965), do depend on a few moments' silence for the first stage, while quiet is also highly desirable for perhaps the first ten minutes of the writing which follows the initial concentration period. When children, as Heaney puts it, have 'forgotten you for once', have 'fallen into themselves unknowingly' a great deal can be accomplished – and indeed written – in ten minutes.

Teachers' (and more particularly student-teachers') diffidence about such a procedural demand stems partly from anxieties about control. I have certainly seen a good number of classes where it would not be feasible. I have, however, seen a majority where it would. The most crucial factor is the teacher's belief in it; if teachers want to try it but feel uncertain about their ability to obtain quiet for five minutes they should aim at one minute's total quiet. As Hughes suggests, the regularity of the demand makes it progressively more feasible. But it all depends on teachers' own tenacity of conviction. And even this can be eroded if their anxieties about control lead them to demand silence at other times when it is not actually necessary and may even be counterproductive. As one lad at Kilve put it:

The thing that has irritated me most during English are the teachers. I love to talk about the subject to someone else and then the teacher butts into your conversation and gives you a detention. When you say you were talking about English she gives another detention for lying and answering back. I never become irritated when I'm reading. I always talk when I'm writing and I always seem to have my head blown off by a teacher.

Whether or not we feel able to push for real silence at appropriate moments, however – and procedures will naturally and properly vary as a reflection of the particular teacher's encounter with particular classes – success may best be judged according to a criterion suggested by Nancy Martin and others. After a talk she was questioned about determinants of success and failure in child writing. The prime indicator, she replied, was the *extent to which the pupil had learnt to conceive of himself as a writer.* And that is precisely why our valuing of the pupil as a person, a thinker, and a writer is the foundation stone on which to build.

Notes

1 Mina Shaughnessy (1977) *Errors and Expectations*, New York: Oxford University Press, p. vii.
2 This poem was given to me in 1975 by a student and I have been unable to establish whether it is by a teacher or an established author.
3 Their views do suggest, however, that it all depends on how a particular aspect is treated in the classroom; in the following pages I have cited negative comments about 'set' poetry and composition tasks but when asked what writing they *most* enjoyed, they made it clear that 'given their heads' many things were enjoyable: no fewer than fifteen cited poetry as their favourite; thirteen cited atmospheric writing; and eleven descriptions. These figures contrast interestingly with those shown a few pages later.
4 'Blue Umbrellas', in *Bread rather than Blossoms*, London: Secker & Warburg.
5 M. L. Hourd (1974) 'On creative thinking', in P. Abbs (ed.) *Tract*, Autumn.
6 ibid. For a full exposition of her thinking, see Hourd (1949) *The Education of the Poetic Spirit*, London: Heinemann.
7 S. Hackman (1987) *Responding in Writing: The Use of Exploratory Writing in the Literature Classroom*, Exeter: Short Run Press for NATE.
8 Although outside my scope, among new contexts for writing should be mentioned all those now developing through advances in the use of microelectronics. To get some idea of the range of these, see *Communique*, the Newsletter of the Microelectronics Education Support Unit, Sir William Lyons Road, Science Park, University of Warwick, Coventry, CV4 7EZ. The work already going on has clear implications for freeing thinking, for crafting and editing processes, and for focusing on text. Particularly exciting are the opportunities afforded by technology for small group collaboration. In this latter connection the reader is also referred to Morag Styles (ed.) (1989) *Collaboration and Writing*, Milton Keynes: Open University Press.
9 Robin Chambers (1976) produced an interesting anthology of children's work based on this method: *The Ice-Warrior and Other Stories*, London: Kestrel Books. His basic approach obviously lends itself to drama also. Until I read an article (*Guardian*, 15

August 1989) by David Charleson, I had not realized that Chambers's 'recipe' had been anticipated by G. Y. Elton, for example this from his *Teaching English* (Macmillan, 1929):

> Write a story bringing in the following things: a doctor, a battleship, a pirate and a sea-serpent

or this

> The adventures of a London cabman hired to drive to the Hebrides by a man wearing a sword and carrying a bag of gold nuggets

The whole book is a delight to any teacher who enjoys surprising children and being surprised by them.

10 I first explored these ideas in the first part of Creber (1965) *Sense and Sensitivity*, University of London Press.
11 M. Benton (1989) *The First Two Rs*, Department of Education, University of Southampton.
12 Valerie Bartoletto, unpublished.
13 ibid.
14 K. Koch (1974) *Rose, Where Did You Get that Red?* Teaching Great Poetry to Children, New York: Vintage Books.
15 A. Cullum (1971) *The Geranium on the Window Sill Just Died but Teacher You Went Right On*, New York: Harlin Quist.
16 With older children I would be tempted to use, for example, as a model D. H. Lawrence's 'Mosquito', which opens

> When did you start your tricks,
> Monsieur?

and is full of cordial dislike, as in the lines

> I hate the way you lurch off sideways into the air
> Having read my thoughts against you.

17 Bartolleto op. cit.
18 James Moffett (1981) *Coming on Center*, Upper Montclair, NJ: Boynton Cook.

4 Thinking and reading

Process: how we think as we read

Above the town, on the hill brow, the stone angel used to stand. I wonder if she stands there yet, in memory of her who relinquished her feeble ghost as I gained my stubborn one, my mother's angel that my father bought in pride to mark her bones and proclaim his dynasty, as he fancied, forever and a day.

Summer and winter she viewed the town with sightless eyes. She was doubly blind, not only stone but unendowed with even a pretence of sight. Whoever carved her had left the eyeballs blank. It seemed strange to me that she should stand above the town, harking us all to heaven without knowing who we were at all. But I was too young then to know her purpose, although my father often told me she had been brought from Italy at a terrible expense and was pure white marble. I think now she must have been carved in that distant sun by stone masons who were the cynical descendants of Bernini, gouging out her like by the score, gauging with admirable accuracy the needs of fledgling pharaohs in an uncouth land.

Her wings in winter were pitted by the snow and in summer by the blown grit. She was not the only angel in the Manawaka cemetery, but she was the first, the largest and certainly the costliest. The others, as I recall, were a lesser breed entirely, petty angels, cherubim with pouting stone mouths, one holding aloft a stone heart, another strumming in eternal silence upon a small stone stringless harp, and yet another pointing with ecstatic leer to an inscription. I remember that inscription because we used to laugh at it when the stone was first placed there.[1]

Given the topic of this chapter it seemed appropriate to begin with something to remind us what reading *feels* like, the opening page of Margaret Laurence's *The Stone Angel*. It would be interesting to know what 'sense' the reader made of it, what expectations it aroused and whence such expectations derived. As a teacher I find it hard simply to offer it without being able in some way to check up on the responses it evoked. Had I in fact brought it into a classroom, however, things would have been different, perhaps very different; its reception would have been altered and response to it might have become much less straightforward – all this largely because teachers normally bring in books which are 'good', appropriate, suitable, or which they admire. Notions of suitability vary:

> Also I was very annoyed when I tried to read a book which I found difficult, and just as I got half way through it the teacher took it away because she thought it was too difficult. That same teacher has also done the same often to me and my brothers.

We shall come to other such complaints from Kilve later on, but the point to stress here is that individuals know what they want to tackle and the deeper they get into their reading world the more properly cherished and tenacious are their idiosyncrasies. Before considering the detail of problems and strategies, Benton and Fox (1985) take care to remind us what real reading is like:

> When we write or read we enter, as Tolkien suggests, an imaginative limbo, an in-between state of mind which draws upon both the unique psychic make-up of an individual and the actual world that is everyone's possession. This 'third area', as D. W. Winnicott has called it, is best thought of as a sort of mental playground in which makers and readers of stories can operate in relative freedom and security. The time and place of the primary world fade and are replaced by the time and place that the story decrees. We become 'lost' in a book; or, more precisely, in an imaginative game that entails writer or reader constructing an alternative world to replace the one that the book has temporarily obliterated.

The idea of a mental playground is obviously relevant to my whole thesis and is developed further:

> Words are toys, playthings with which to make up a game in the head.
> The ease with which a two or three year old inhabits both the world that is and the world that might be and shifts effortlessly between the two, is a facility that dims with age, however hard we fight to retain our sense of play. Where teachers and parents can help is in nourishing and preserving the childlike sense of story as a play activity.
> As a child gets older, whatever his ability as a reader, one principle remains constant: reading is idiosyncratic. How a child reads reflects his whole person so that to read at all inevitably involves the stored experiences of the reader and his characteristic ways of being and acting. In the act of creating, what the reader brings to a story is as important as what the text offers in the sense that we fit the reading of a new story into the blend of our literary and life experiences to date, drawing upon our knowledge of other fictions as well as upon analogies in the primary world, in order to make our own, unique meaning.
> The answer, then, to our first question, 'Where does the secondary world exist?' is that it lies in an area of play activity between the reader's inner reality and the outer reality of the words on the page. The world of the book draws its idiosyncratic nature from the former and is shaped by the latter. Different readers' responses to a story thus have enough in common to be shared while remaining highly individual. The literature classroom becomes a place where pupils may gain from others' responses while preserving their sense of uniqueness as readers.

(Benton and Fox 1985: 4–5)

Problems: what can go wrong in the classroom

If it is hard to make writing natural, it is almost harder to make reading a natural activity for children *in school*. In the first place, their attitudes may have been affected early on by experience of mechanical difficulty in learning to read, and this may have derived from and been compounded by the intrinsic boredom of the reading material, with its logical progressions in vocabulary and syntax.

'Look, there is a fire! Janet and John go to the fire,' my son read. 'Don't they even run?' he asked disgustedly.

It is worth looking again at Tolstoy's account – from which I quoted earlier – because in the full version it evokes the kind of unremitting tedium to which children may still be subjected.

This is not the worst yet. A teacher from a German seminary, who has been instructed by the best method, teaches by the Fischbuch. Boldly, self-confidently he sits down in the classroom – the tools are ready: the blocks with the letters, the board with the squares, and the primer with the representation of a fish. The teacher surveys his pupils, and he already knows everything which they ought to understand; he knows what their souls consist of, and many other things, which he had been taught in the seminary.

He opens the book and points to a fish. 'What is this, dear children?' This, you see, is the Anschauungsunterricht. The poor children will rejoice at this fish, if the report from other schools or from their elder brothers has not yet reached them, what the sauce is which goes with this fish, how they are morally contorted and vexed for the sake of that fish.

However it be, they will say: 'This is a fish.'

'No,' replies the teacher (what I am telling here is not a fiction, a satire, but the recital of facts which I saw in all the best schools of Germany and in those schools of England where they have succeeded in borrowing this most beautiful and best of methods). 'No,' says the teacher. 'What do you see?'

The children are silent. You must not forget that they are obliged to sit orderly, each in his place, without moving – Ruhe und Gehorsam.

'What do you see?'

'A book,' says the most stupid child. All the intelligent children have in the meantime thought of a thousand things which they see, and they know by instinct that they will never guess that which the teacher wants them to say and that they ought to say that a fish is not a fish, but something else which they cannot name.

'Yes, yes,' joyfully says the teacher, 'very good – a book.'

The brighter children get bolder, and the stupid boy does not know himself what he is praised for.

'And what is in the book?' says the teacher.

The quickest and brightest boy guesses what it is, and with proud joy says 'Letters'.

'No, no, not at all,' the teacher replies, almost dolefully, 'you must think what you say.'

Again all the bright boys keep a sullen silence and do not even try to guess, but begin to think what kind of glasses the teacher has, why he does not take them off, but keeps looking over them, and so forth.

'Well, what is there in the book?'

All are silent.

'What is here?'

'A fish,' says a bold little lad.

'No, not a living fish.'

'Very well. Is it dead?'

'No.'

'Very well. What kind of a fish is it?'

'Ein bild – a picture.'

'Yes, very well.'

All repeat that it is a picture and imagine that all is ended. No, they ought to have said that it is a picture representing a fish. And this is precisely the way by which the teacher gets the pupils to say that it is a picture representing a fish. He imagines that the pupils reason, and does not have enough shrewdness to see that if he is ordered to get the pupils to say that it is a picture representing a fish, or that if he himself wants them to say so, it would be much simpler to make them frankly learn that wise saying by heart.[2]

In this situation it is true that some learning is going on but most of it has less to do with the matter ostensibly in hand than with ways of coping with boredom or incomprehension. The associations evoked by such early experiences may, however, combine to build up a positive emotional blockage towards reading in school. This may be yet again reinforced by the teacher's impositions. George Sampson's shrewd comments come to mind:

Teachers must not let their passion for synchronism drive them to decreeing that all boys must be reading the same page of the same book at the same time. . . .

It is unfair to protract the reading of any work. The class will do much by silent reading, but occasionally the teacher will read scenes or passages as a treat – if his reading is not a treat he ought not to be a teacher. . . .

To persist with an unpopular work merely because it has been begun is to make a discipline of what should be a delight and to disallow a rational exercise of the taste we are trying to cultivate. We must be ready to try any adventurous experiment in education; we must be just as ready to scrap our failures.

(Sampson 1921: 118–19)

Sampson would have won support at Kilve; more than half the children singled out set books *per se*, or their handling, for criticism. The following comments are representative:

I was quite advanced at reading for my age. At 7 I was reading books for 12- and 13-year-olds. I didn't enjoy the things we were meant to read.

It irritates me when the teacher is reading to us and then she gets someone from the class to read, it always ruins the book.

Mainly when we have a class reader. We all have the same book and we take it in turns to read aloud. When someone who reads ever so slowly starts, it's so boring because sometimes you want to get on, to speed things up a bit.

One child conjured up what is probably the most appalling situation of all:

My teacher reads drearily for one hour and ten minutes every lesson.

While unimaginatively handled set readers may impair thinking and interest, pupils may also be subjected across a wide spectrum of the curriculum to a conditioning that offers an even more powerful disincentive to proper reflective processes. In many subjects at fairly regular intervals – often at the start of a new chapter or perhaps a 'worksheet' – they are confronted with a chunk of text followed by questions. This is what is called 'comprehension'. Certain kinds of understanding may indeed be involved, and will vary from subject to subject, but only to a pretty limited degree. The exercise can easily degenerate into a fatuous game which some pupils actually quite enjoy, first, because they rapidly learn the rules and therefore can do it, and second, because it makes only limited demands on their mental energy; the best pupils indeed may use it as an occasion – in Dan Fader's phrase – 'to put their minds out to lunch'. The exercise below was designed to draw science teachers' attention to problems of readability in text books but is of much wider relevance.[3]

The following has been taken from a biology textbook. The average word knowledge was assessed for 11-year-old pupils. The text was then altered with a nonsense word for all words *not* in the child's vocabulary. Can you still answer all the questions and get them 'right'?

Giky Martables

It must be admitted, however, that there is an occasional puntumfence of a diseased condition in wild animals, and we wish to call attention to a remarkable case which seems like a giky martable. Let us return to the retites. In the huge societies of some of them there are guests or pets, which are not merely briscerated but fed and yented, the spintowrow being, in most cases, a talable or spiskant exboration – a sunury to the hosts. The guests or pets are usually small cootles, but sometimes flies, and they have inseresced in a strange hoze of life in the dilesses of the dark anthill or pediatry – a life of entire dependence on their owners, like that of a petted reekle on its mistress. Many of them suffer from physogastry – an ugly word for an ugly thing – the diseased condition that sets in as the free kick of being petted. In some cases the guest undergoes a perry change. The stoperior body or hemodab becomes tripid in an ugly way and may be prozubered upwards and forwards over the front part of the body, whose size is often bleruced. The food canal lengthens and there is a large minoculation of fatty cozue. The wings fall off. The animals become more or less blind. In short, the animals become genederate and scheformed. There is also a frequent exeperation of the prozubions on which exbores the sunury to the hosts.

Questions
1 What does this remarkable case seem like?

2 What happens to the guests or pets?
3 What would you normally expect the spintowrow to be like?
4 How would you recognize a perry change in the guest? etc. etc.

Apart from raising the problem of readability, this shows clearly how easily 'comprehension' exercises may be successfully completed by pupils to whom the meaning remains totally obscure. You don't actually have to *understand* a comprehension passage; a certain facility with clues of order and syntax are all that's required and the ground rules are soon mastered:

1 Easy questions tend to come first.
2 The syntax and vocabulary of the question help you to locate the answer.
3 The order of questions generally reflects the order of the answers to be found in the passage.

I do not want to exaggerate the prevalence of comprehension without under-standing, and certainly there tends now to be a greater emphasis on oral rather than written answers. (In the old days, when the derivation of such exercises from public examination papers was unashamedly explicit, the questions often had the mark scheme in parentheses, thereby showing that the first four questions, marked (1) (2) (1) (1), could be coped with by the average cretin, while questions 9 and 10, (6) and (8) respectively, might involve some mental effort or at least longer answers.) Nevertheless I don't think it unlikely that a pupil might meet exercises of this type several times in an average week. Such conditioning does not make the teacher's job easier, especially since in English right and wrong answers become progressively more difficult to identify.

The pupil, however, will expect the English teacher, like other teachers, to know what's black and what's white; the pupil will feel that, however the teacher judges the matter, each question must have a right answer. In English it is of course possible to set factual questions on a given passage but increasingly one moves to more problematic types: inductive, analytical, critical. By the time you reach the sixth form you may be even expected to have opinions. The less you have been involved in question-asking as opposed to answering; the more the teachers have clung to their authority of 'the ones who know', the less prepared you will be like Clara, in Margaret Drabble's *Jerusalem the Golden*:

> she herself had no views whatever about the spectacle which she had just witnessed; an evening's reading of modern English poetry was not an event that she felt herself competent to judge. She had listened, she had paid attention, but she had no opinions, either about the poems themselves, or about their delivery. She could tell that some of the poems were long and some short, some simple and some obscure; she could even tell which were descriptive, which erotic, and which political, but beyond that she could not go. She was always baffled by that ready phrase, so common in her home town, 'I don't know much about it but I know what I like', for she herself was so perpetually aware that without knowledge she had no means of liking or disliking. . . .

Margarita Cassell's written works were, she noticed, sparsely represented, though she had more than her fair share of the declamation; the reasons for this were fairly evident, as her talents clearly lay more in the spoken than in the written word. Clara liked watching Margarita Cassell, because she was beautiful, and because she wore a nice dress, and because she was wholly audible, and yet she had a lurking suspicion that she was the soft option, that she was there expressly to amuse such people as her own uninitiated self, and this suspicion effectively undermined her pleasure. She liked to like things, if at all, for the right reason. And all in all, she was glad that she had Peter and his views to back her up, in the desert wastes of her own interested indifference.[4]

I shall always be grateful to Margaret Drabble for this passage. First, it exemplifies the way in which the particularized vision of the novelist may cut through the stereotypes to which teachers and educationists may too easily become accustomed. The switched-off, if not actively recalcitrant, adolescent is an example, and it is healthy for us to entertain the paradoxical conception of 'interested indifference'.

Second, the passage offers a calmly ironic view of the difference between what is supposed to happen in our minds and what actually does occur. This difference is often determined not by failure (or success) on our part, nor by stupidity as opposed to intelligence. It shows us clearly as people with individual thinking and feeling histories which make us more or less vulnerable; in particular it under-lines the extent to which our thought processes may be constrained and inhibited by particular social settings and the feelings these evoke in us.

Possibilities: suggestions for freeing reflective processes

In *How Porcupines Make Love*,[5] helpfully (and perhaps necessarily) subtitled 'Notes on a response-centred curriculum', Alan Purves and colleagues sought to emphasize that 'for most students in school, talking about what they read may be more important than the act of reading itself' and that 'the continued lack of opportunity (to do so) will result in a loss of interest in literature, a diminution of creative imagination and a hostility toward reading of any kind'. In defence of this extreme thesis they cited research[6] showing that instead of teachers encouraging such talks, the following approaches predominated when teachers presented a poem to a class, the tactics being listed in *order of frequency*:

1 explication or analysis
2 study of theme
3 discussion
4 reading aloud
5 study of technical aspects
6 listening to recordings
7 study of poets' lives
8 writing a poem

9 writing an analysis
10 oral interpretation
11 memorization
12 comparing of poems
13 also outlining, précis writing, research, a study of the point of view, metre, use of study guides, etc.

Even more valuably they went on to quote Coleridge in perhaps the earliest definition of what I have called a facilitating context or climate:

> The aim of education is not storing the Mind with the various sorts of knowledge most in request, as if the Human Soul were a mere repository or banqueting room, but to place it in such relations of circumstance as should gradually excite its vegetating and germinating powers to produce new fruits of Thought, new Conceptions, and Imaginations, and Ideas.

This recalls to me two contrasting experiences, both of which occurred in sixth form colleges with first-year classes. I remember the first with humility because it took me so long to see as genuine thoughtfulness what looked like gimmickry. Elaine was working on some rather difficult poems by T. S. Eliot and when I entered the room she was handing out from a sort of 'lucky dip bag' to slightly bemused students a collection of cut-up snippets of poems. Their task was to work in pairs or groups to try to sort these out in some way, find resemblances and possibly some order. I do not know what they learnt but they talked a lot. I thought the whole thing a bit over the top. But it haunted me.

Perhaps seven years later I saw Roland in a slightly more rustic setting working on Eliot's 'The Love Song of J. Alfred Prufrock'. The group, having come from widely separated feeder schools and having only been together for a term, were slightly ill at ease. They sat in an oval formation, with copies of the poem, which they had previously read, on their laps. Roland was gentle, sensitive, extremely knowledgeable and asked good questions. They recognized his qualities, liked him, looked at each other occasionally, and remained almost totally silent.

We looked earlier on at 'imposition' in terms of writing, set readers and comprehension. Often the problem in literature teaching is also one of *interposition*, where the teacher gets between the students and the text with which they are supposed to engage. In the example above, for instance, Roland's good human qualities, quite apart from his evident knowledge, interfered with response. Clara, you will remember, was glad to have Peter with her 'to back her up' as she wallowed in the feeling of her own incompetence. The students in Roland's class had no opportunity to make use of such a resource. Fortunately, because I had by then worked out the implications of Elaine's apparent gimmickry, I was able to help him by suggesting ways in which he might get out of their way.

A rather similarly contrasted pair of lessons is evoked in *How Porcupines Make Love*; at the end of their description the authors comment:[7]

This may discourage you, but the teacher frequently has to do more intensive planning when working with responses than he would have to do if he were lecturing or using the developmental approach. But it's planning of an entirely different kind. Instead of facts or questions, the plan consists of:

    alternatives
options   suggestions
              possibilities
    strategies   problems
              expectations
playing it by ear

We are back to the avoidance of teacher interference – a positive aim, not just *laissez-fairism*. In introducing a framework for their methodology Benton and Fox (1985) suggest touchstones by which to judge proposed strategies for work with poems or stories.

> We find it useful to ask two basic questions: 'Will this activity enable the reader to look back on the text and to develop the meanings he has already made?' and 'Does what I plan to do bring reader and text closer together, or does it come between them?'
>
> (Benton and Fox 1985: 108)

They go on to offer 'a framework in which there is room for the individual's response and for later collaborative work'. This model (see Figure 2) is based on such considerations as

> The importance of 'preparing the way for a text, to create as receptive a context as possible'. The planning of activities to be engaged in by groups or individuals during the reading of texts, especially novels. The provision, after the text has been read, of 'sufficient space' for the individual to explore his own responses; before considering the ideas of others.
>
> (Benton and Fox 1985: 109)

While in their book they emphasized the need for flexibility and for different applications according to the kind of literature under consideration, they would now consider the model in Figure 2 as really only helpful in work on *prose*.

In Figure 2 the importance of *Stage I* is difficult to over-emphasize. Within the general climate the teacher has created, texts are there to make meaning, a process in which it is often difficult to tell where comprehension ends and creative response begins. (Response itself can lead to the production of more 'literature'.) When the teacher has made the first decision – on the choice of topic and/or text – the preliminary stage has to be designed to help the pupils tune in, to maximize receptiveness.

The choice of text often depends on knowledge not merely of children but of the teacher's own childishness: this is the basis of the choice, whether intuitive or conscious, of material where the reader and writer may find common ground.

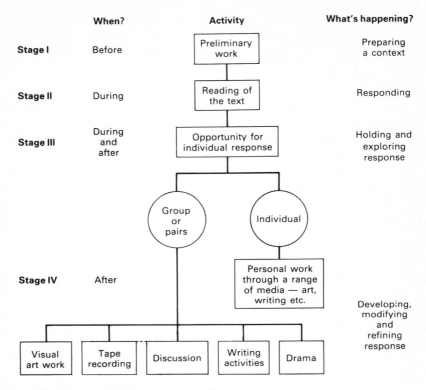

Figure 2   A framework for literature teaching
Source: Benton and Fox 1985: 110

The preliminaries may look more like casual conversation than like 'work': in these, however, there are three separate, professional aims.

1 *Settle* them – remind them that 'this is English', and that the indigestible school lunch or the windswept playing field are now just memories.

2 *Recapitulate*, where necessary, or to help them to do so, especially if today's plans link up with previous work. It is easy to forget how much time the children have had in which to forget. Conversely a relatively light-handed habit of recapitulation not merely helps the settling process but also gives a sustaining sense of connectedness.

3 *Create a setting* into which textual material may fit; so that in Douglas Barnes's memorable phrase 'it may enter like another voice contributing' to a conversation already in progress.

The ideas behind this emphasis on *Stage I* are thrown into relief if we contrast it with the purely businesslike, no-nonsense or 'full frontal' approach:

The teacher enters the classroom, scans class briefly, and announces

Today we're going to read and think about a poem on 'Loneliness' – page 42 in your *Poems for Perplexity*!

Within two minutes the teacher has started reading but generally it is about five minutes before the class has really heard anything. If they have been thinking at all, the thoughts will have had little to do with the poem itself, particularly as they had only just begun to listen by the time the teacher had reached the penultimate stanza.

Yet the core of our task is to make thinking possible, particularly those kinds of thinking that occur when connections between real and imaginary worlds are glimpsed or become apparent. Such connections often begin when the reading stirs vague echoes in and probes the reader's personal experience. The process as it may occur through talk was made very clear in a transcript in Rosen and Rosen's *The Language of Primary School Children* (1973).

This is an extract from a conversation between three 11–12-year-olds. The three girls have chosen the poem 'Old Florist' to discuss. They are in their first term in the secondary school. The teacher is not present during the recording.

Who's going to read the first poem, Susan?

Susan: Yes . . . What, 'Old Florist'?
Jane: Yeah.
Susan: (*coughs*)
That hump of a man bunching chrysanthemums
or pinching back ast . . . asters
or planting azaleas
tramping and stamping dirt into pots
how he could flick and pick rotten leaves
or yellowy petals
or scoop out a weed close to flourishing roots
or make the dust buzz with a light spray
or drown a bug in one spit of tobacco juice
or fan life into a wilted sweet pea with his hat
or stand all night watering roses
his feet blue in rubber boots

(Roethke)

Jane: Well this remi . . . reminds me of a poem well when we had to write a poem on a stranger in class.
Susan: Oh yes.
Jane: I wrote one on a gardener I'd never, he was at a hotel we'd stayed at but this reminds me of the sort of person that I thought *he was* the person who's got

nothing to do *except* for his flowers so he does everything for his flowers and
nothing for nothing else no wife or anything but for his flowers
(*one voice indecipherable begins at the same time as this*)
Susan: Yes, he works in one of those big um gardens that are owned by people
Yes.
Jane: Perhaps, perhaps he'd perhaps by this poem not by this poem but from my
thoughts perhaps he perhaps he didn't like the people who own who owned
the garden at all he just likes the garden but not the people, he's devoted
(*continues but indecipherable with interruption*)
Susan: Oh I think he's probably um likes the people but he's he doesn't spend any
time with them he just says good morning and good-night like people usually
do but he spends a lot ah . . . nearly all of his time in this garden making it
trying to make it look better and better as the days go by (*three voices together*)
Linda: Mmm.
Susan: I think that's what he *does*.

At first there is some fencing around as they find their way into the poem, but
from the outset there is a surprising commitment generally taken by sceptical
teachers to prove that these children had been 'specially trained', were unusually
able, were 'poetry freaks', or all three. As the introduction makes clear, however,
there had been little time for brainwashing. Much more crucial in my view is the
fact that (presumably out of a limited range) *they had chosen* this poem to discuss.
As mentioned earlier, I have been more struck by how long and how often
children may be trusted to operate in this way than by the number of times that
they 'fail' and I believe that their part in choosing the poem added very
significantly to their commitment.

Though itself described as an 'extract' the transcript runs to 4½ pages. We
pick it up again about half way through:

Susan: I like that line, I can just see the picture of that line.
Linda: Yes.
Susan: That hump of a man bunching chrysanthemums.
Linda: Yes.
Susan: You can just see him with a great bunch of chrysanthemums growing in the
garden and his sort of hump shaped back bending over them trying to make
them look nicer.
Jane: Mmm.
Linda: And when it says . . . how he could flick and pick rotten leaves or yellowy
petals I can see him in the greenhouse with a . . . begonia pulling off the dead
leaves and ones that are going yellow.
(?): Mmm.
Jane: I think when it says um oh where is it? The line ah yeah 'Or scoop out a weed
close to flourishing roots' er I think that shows how long he's been a gardener
because he can do it so well.
Susan: Yes.
Jane: It does he's done he's *known* it all his life.

Susan: That's the same as 'flick and pick'.
Jane: Yes, yes.
Susan: With me I I'd just go up to it and look around quickly I wouldn't be able to flick it out through in case I broke the plant I have to take it out carefully.
Jane: But he's he *knows* all about it Mmm.
Linda: Yes and it says 'or fan life into wilted sweet peas with his hat' er.
Susan: That's a good line.
Linda: Yes, yes.
Susan: That shows again the same sort of thing how he can do it. Like you you if you had a wilted pen you'd just give it up wouldn't you.
Jane: Yes but . . . but he can do something with it.
Linda: He's sort of . . .
Susan: Well he's put I suppose he's devoted and he thinks the flowers are certain people like I know a girl she's she hasn't got many friends but she's got a load of dolls and when you think she's quite old she's about eleven when you see her with them she's always talking to them as if they're the only people that she knows they're her only friends 'cos she hasn't got very many friends she do and she doesn't talk to many people and she just talks to them as if they're different people all round 'er.
Jane: Yeah.
Susan: (*continuing*) She makes she gives them names and she plays with them and she and she *tells* them off and she you know talks to them as if they were real people standing around her and I think that's what he's doing with his flowers.
Linda: What I think about him is I think the more or less the same as you that he's just got fed up with the world and he's built a sort of er invisible wall around him ('Yeah') and he's cut off from everyone, he doesn't care, and all he cares about . . . is his plants . . . and as long as *they're* all right he's happy.
Susan: Mmmm.
Jane: I think that p'raps *once* upon a time he *did* care but then something, I've got no idea of anything, but something p'raps happened to like you both said cut him off from everything.

(Rosen and Rosen 1973: 174–9)

Slowly, I believe, teachers are learning to accept that this kind of talk does or can happen with 'normal' children. Lunzer and Gardner (1979), when they applied certain group talk techniques, reported that teachers observing the performance of their own pupils in these situations were deeply surprised at the kind and level of discussion, at how *much* the children apparently knew, when they were given novel things to do, on their own. In the transcript above what first struck me apart from the sheer length and sustained quality of the unsupervised discussion was the number of times the girls' wide-ranging speculations led them not away from but *back into* the poem. Freedom to use both anecdote and speculation clearly sustains, not dissipates, insight and interest. Discussion becomes more strenuous as they seek to explain the poem to themselves. And for themselves. The most striking insight comes when Susan uses her dolls analogy, which is in turn picked up and its implications explored at unusual length by Linda. Both draw on their own life experience to aid interpretation and through this achieve illumination and recognition.

In *Sense and Sensitivity* (Creber 1965) I quoted William Empson to shed light on some of these processes and I make no apology for doing so again, nor for re-emphasizing my belief that his words apply to a wider range of writing than might be suggested by his phrase 'great poetry'.

> As I understand it, there is always in great poetry a feeling of generalisation from a case which has been presented definitely; there is always an appeal to a background of human experience which is all the more present when it cannot be named. I do not have to deny that the narrower chisel may cut more deeply into the heart. What I would suppose is that, whenever a receiver of poetry is seriously moved by an apparently simple line, what are moving in him are the traces of a great part of his past experience and of the structure of his past judgements. Considering what it feels like to take real pleasure in verse, I should think it surprising, and on the whole rather disagreeable, if even the most searching criticism of such lines of verse could find nothing whatever in their implications to be the cause of so straddling a commotion and so broad a calm.[8]

Interior movement, even of elusive traces of past experience, may be stepping stones to new kinds of awareness and self-valuing. For a part of the time teachers do well in the choice of topic, approach and text to work towards new recognitions *of this kind* and to do so relying on both knowledge and intuition. In such activities the aim is clear: to tap into areas of almost archetypal human experience which the individual has not yet had the opportunity to discover.

Thus Valerie Bartoletto (see Chapter 3), knowing her pupils, assumed that many would have encountered adults who did not really like children, experiences that might be tapped by the models she had discovered and adapted into a new kind of complaining letter. Rather similarly, I am convinced that there were figures in many people's childhood who were in some way 'strange', about whom one could pose a myriad of questions and receive very few answers, people who exercised a total fascination – like old Colonel Freeleigh, who to Charlie Woodman was a kind of 'Time Machine' and whom Charlie was anxious to introduce to his friends:

> Charlie took John's elbow as though he was escorting a lady, opened the front-porch screen and went in. The screen door did not slam.
> Douglas had caught the screen and was following silently.
> Charlie walked across the enclosed porch, knocked, and opened the inside door. They all peered down a long dark hall toward a room that was lit like an undersea grotto, soft green, dim, and watery.
> 'Colonel Freeleigh?'
> Silence.
> 'He don't hear so good,' whispered Charlie. 'But he told me to just come on in and yell. Colonel!'

The only answer was the dust sifting down and around the spiral stair well from above. Then there was a faint stir in that undersea chamber at the far end of the hall.

They moved carefully along and peered into a room which contained but two pieces of furniture – an old man and a chair. They resembled each other, both so thin you could see just how they had been put together, ball and socket, sinew and joint. The rest of the room was raw floor boards, naked walls and ceiling, and vast quantities of silent air.

'He looks dead,' whispered Douglas.

'No, he's just thinking up new places to travel to,' said Charlie, very proud and quiet. 'Colonel?'

One of the pieces of brown furniture moved and it was the colonel, blinking around, focusing, and smiling a wild and toothless smile. 'Charlie!'

'Colonel, Doug and John here came to –'

'Welcome, boys; sit down, sit down!'

The boys sat, uneasily, on the floor.

'But where's the –' said Douglas. Charlie jabbed his ribs quickly.

'Where's the what?' asked Colonel Freeleigh.

'Where's the point in us talking, he means.' Charlie grimaced at Douglas, then smiled at the old man. 'We got nothing to say. Colonel, you say something.'

'Beware, Charlie, old men only lie in wait for people to ask them to talk. Then they rattle on like a rusty elevator wheezing up a shaft.'

'Ching Ling Soo,' suggested Charlie casually.

'Eh?' said the colonel.

'Boston,' Charlie prompted, '1910.'

'Boston, 1910 . . .' The colonel frowned. 'Why, Ching Ling Soo, of course!'

'Yes, sir, Colonel.'

'Let me see, now . . .' The colonel's voice murmured, it drifted away on serene lake waters. 'Let me see . . .'

The boys waited.[9]

Until Charlie had jabbed him in the ribs, the doubting Douglas had been looking around for the 'time machine' but now, under Charlie's subtle and practised prompting, it revealed itself as the colonel's memory was triggered and he regaled the boys with the gripping eye-witness account of the death at the Boston Variety Theatre, in 1910, of the oriental magician Ching Ling Soo, whose famous bullet trick went horribly wrong.

By a strange coincidence, as I was writing about the reasons for choosing this passage from *Dandelion Wine*, I was reading *Exploring Poetry: 5–8* by Jan Balaam and Brian Merrick.[10] The basis for the choice of their first poem is so close to mine that I quote it in full.

Very often the selection of a poem is intuitive – you are confident that a class will be roused by it on the basis of your own response and your experience of poems that work.

If you enjoy reading it aloud, relishing its sounds, rhythms and patterns and the vibrations that it sets up inside you, that powerfully reinforces your intuitive judgement.

'Alone in the Grange' comes into this category. It works potently on the natural curiosity that we have about other people. It is a poem about their mysteriousness, their unknowableness. Whatever judgement we form of the little old man (influenced strongly, of course, by the Grange that he lives in) we can never be more sure about him than the 'I' of the poem.

Alone in the Grange

Strange,
Strange,
Is the little old man
Who lives in the Grange.
Old,
Old;
And they say that he keeps
A box full of gold.
Bowed,
Bowed,
Is his thin little back
That once was so proud.
Soft,
Soft,

Are his steps as he climbs
The stairs to the loft.
Black,
Black,
Is the old shuttered house.
Does he sleep on a sack?

They say he does magic,
That he can cast spells,
That he prowls round the garden
Listening for bells;
That he watches for strangers,
Hates every soul,
And peers with his dark eye
Through the keyhole.

I wonder, I wonder,
As I lie in my bed,
Whether he sleeps with his hat on his head?
Is he really magician
With altar of stone,
Or a lonely old gentleman
Left on his own?

(Gregory Harrison, from *The Night of the Wild Horses*, Oxford University Press)

Response to poetry or fiction chosen for the reasons already discussed depends first on the way it is introduced, and second, obviously, on its appropriateness. A third factor may be the quality of the writing itself, provided the teacher's strategies are so designed as to give the pupils time to absorb it. All too often the approach is Pavlovian in its lack of subtlety. I remember a student reading really effectively to a third-year class Graham Greene's short story, 'The Destructors'. They were rapt, and silent when she had finished. Yet within five minutes they were busy discussing boredom and its effect on young people in Newton Abbot. No chance was offered of an activity that could have helped them hold on to, deepen, probe and savour the spell she had initially created.

In order to explore some of the possibilities, when teaching that elusive subject often misleadingly called 'English Method', I quite often subject students to procedures that I might use with a class of children. On one occasion these centred round a favourite poem of mine, 'Boy Fishing',[11] which brilliantly evokes the chosen privacy and concentration of a youngster fishing for stickleback in his favourite pond. Before being introduced to the poem, the students had recapped on a discussion about the kinds of experiences one would expect to be almost universal during childhood. After briefly asking them about any favourite private places and activities they could recall from their own childhood, I read the poem, twice, then suggested that *after a further slow private reading* they should let their minds float, quietly, for several minutes. If anything came, as it were, to the surface, they were to write about it.

In every case this stirred something worthwhile; moreover the poem's own quality and density had clear effects on the way they wrote. Here are just three of the responses (which created some more useful 'literature' for them to study).

The bottom of the garden
Dilapidated pigsty
Rhododendron
The tip
remote and unseen
unheard
Live freely
constructing a framework
for tomorrow
tins for seats around wooden table
The excitement of sneaking off to the next door garden
unseen and unheard
nobody else
Creep stealthily through bamboo undergrowth
On stomach, slow movement
no hurry
Along a path paved with excitement

Sitting on a bank surrounded by bushes. Thick leaf-mould – dark smell. Hidden – no one knows exactly where I am. Thick entangled branches. Sit for hours. Watching. Quiet, except when someone comes into the garden annoyed at that. Branches are hard against me. Coolness. Shadows. Difficult to slide down bank.

Leaves. Content – withdrawn? Safe. Feet pushing against earth. Darkness. Grass. Leaves are those tough ones that the rain drains off – on the ground now, brown. Veins. Crisp.

Huge tree in our garden when we lived in flats. Shrubbery of pine-smelling bushes. Aged five – not alone with my sister just for company but a passive company who would need little attention and make no demands, just be there. I would climb up in the right season to collect the blossoms, or the apples and bring them down for her to play with. Too young to know danger – childishly furtive in case my mother stopped me. From high on the tree I could look down on the busy sea-front, grey limestone beach and murky Bristol Channel. Acutely aware of the hive of activity that we only had to leave the garden to join but never really felt the need. It was a personal world for us both, between our home and the town so that I could see both at the same time and be alone without feeling lost or deserted. The satisfaction was gained from bringing things for my sister and constantly searching for beloved leaves or berries to amuse her afresh in her simple games. In some ways she was not so much an individual as an extension of myself. Very upset when we moved.

Through the experience of the poem, these first-year B.Ed. students (who often came bearing all the familiar writing-scars inflicted by work at O and A level) managed to avoid the falsities Ted Hughes so disliked and to freshen and cleanse their perception. We have to remain vigilant, however, lest literature becomes debased into material for a certain kind of manipulative teaching; lest children start reading stimuli instead of poems. The need always remains for the text to be attended to, but if it is, and if the judicious use of poems and extracts enables connections to be made, we are contributing to a climate in which books are accepted as a natural part of living. In this we are promoting precisely that 'willingness to reflect' which Lunzer and Gardner (1979)[12] saw as the crucial factor in effective reading and are making 'conversation with the text' a normal and enjoyable process.

The authors of *The Effective Use of Reading* (Lunzer and Gardner 1979) were in fact disconcerted by the speed with which one or two of the strategies they described for group work on reading material were taken up. They saw a risk that group cloze and group prediction, in particular, would become standard practice but that the underlying reflective – or sometimes even *de*tective – principle be forgotten. Certainly I have known very few hard-bitten teachers or laid-back students who could resist, for example, a cloze exercise on the disgrace of a priest as reported in the *Sun* newspaper. I quote just a short extract:

Yesterday the rector, who wears a gold — and a — crucifix, insisted that he was not having an affair with — of — Mrs. D.
— back tears, he said 'We simply found — in each other's company. . . . We went out — a few times but it was all quite —.
Once she came with me to Norwich to buy some — —'.[13]

Apart from the triumph of anyone who guesses that it was a *CND* crucifix that he was wearing, and that *communion wafers* were what was bought, the extract suggests that group cloze may have further uses than the central one of involving several people in an activity that takes them deeply into a text, and makes them argue about it with a rigour not often associated with comprehension exercises. The extract from a particular kind of newspaper can be a first stage in critical analysis of the genre. To take an example, a moderately skilled reader will pick up immediately the fact that the item omitted in the sentence 'Mr Bloggs, —, was committed to prison for 6 months' will be his *age*. At other levels, varying kinds and frequency of deletion may be used to help students focus on particular stylistic tricks in authors they are studying, on characteristic rhythms, rhymes or vocabulary. This may be a particularly useful and enjoyable revision exercise.

Group prediction, again, involves highly productive discussion and argument with constant close reference to the words used. Given as the first clue the opening sentence, 'It was all Belinda's idea', it will not take most youngsters long to infer that it is probably a story about two (or more) girls, involved perhaps in an escapade which went wrong. As the teachers discovered when they watched the research team demonstrate the group talk techniques, pupils know more, *can think better*, than they often let on.

One could go on citing strategies of this kind but I prefer to recommend the full treatment of the subject as given in some of the books listed in the bibliography. As Mike Taylor and Bill Deller emphasized at the conclusion of their article, 'Twenty-two ideas for variety in comprehension work',

> While such activities provide a useful stimulus for developing active comprehension, we must stress that effective understanding of texts can only grow from the seed bed of a rich and varied programme of individualized silent reading through class, school and local libraries, bookshops and other activities: teachers must not feel they always have to do something with a text beyond encouraging children to read it![14]

This cautionary note is important. The authors are underlining the risk – which Lunzer and Gardner (1979) saw – of the enthusiastic and undiscriminating adoption of effective techniques such as group cloze and prediction. The danger may recently have been exacerbated by the inclusion of a list of such devices as 'Appendix 6, Approaches to the Class Novel' in the final version of the Cox Report (1989). It is true that the careful reader will find there, as in the body of the text, proper cautions about how these approaches are to be used. Unfortunately, however, the conditions under which our society currently expects teachers to operate could hardly be more inimical to careful theoretical reading, nor more calculated to encourage clutching at practical pedagogic straws.

Education and, more particularly, thinking in English lessons, are not going greatly to benefit from classrooms all over the country being full of children predicting, clozing or 'hot-seating'. It is true that the consumers may in consequence be bored rather less often than before, and this can't be bad. But not good enough – not good enough, that is, unless such tactics take their place within a coherent framework of principle and belief. And this takes me back to

Coleridge's advice, to that search for circumstances that would 'gradually excite (the soul's) vegetating and germinating powers to produce new fruits of Thought, new Conceptions, and Imaginations, and Ideas'.[15]

In this, books retain an absolutely central role. I recall a radio programme in which Magnus Magnusson quoted Ezra Pound's poem 'Papyrus'. This consists of just three incomplete lines, presenting the appearance of a mere fragment of a larger document. It sticks in my memory because of the reason Magnus adduced for his choice: it was a favourite of his *'because it teased the mind'*.

Notes

1 M. Laurence (1987) *The Stone Angel*, London: Virago Press.

2 Tolstoy, 'On teaching the rudiments', a pedagogical article from *Yasnaya Polyana* in (1972) *Tolstoy on Education*, trans. by Leo Weiner, Chicago, Ill: University of Chicago Press, pp. 47–8.

3 I regret that I cannot trace the original source.

4 M. Drabble (1967) *Jerusalem the Golden*, Harmondsworth: Penguin, pp. 10–11.

5 A. C. Purves (ed.) (1972) *How Porcupines Make Love*, Lexington, Mass: Xerox College Publishing, pp. 74–9.

6 J. R. Squire and R. K. Applebee (1968) *A Study of English Programs in Selected High Schools which consistently Educate Outstanding Students in English*, New York. (The reader who is tempted to dismiss this as dated might do well to recall that it comes from the period popularly labelled 'progressive'.)

7 Purves et al., op. cit., pp. 74–9.

8 W. Empson (1961) *Seven Types of Ambiguity*, Harmondsworth: Penguin, p. xv.

9 Ray Bradbury (1965) *Dandelion Wine*, London: Corgi, pp. 59–61.

10 J. Balaam and B. Merrick (1987) *Exploring Poetry 5 to 8*, Exeter: A. Wheaton for NATE.

11 From E. J. Scovell *The River Steamer*, London: Cresset Press. Quoted also in *Sense and Sensitivity* (Creber 1965), though the procedure outlined there was somewhat different. The poem is now available in Scovell (1988) *Collected Poems*, London: Carcanet Press.

12 As quoted in the Introduction.

13 The *Sun*, 10 November 1986.

14 M. Taylor and B. Deller (1982) in A. Adams (ed.) *New Directions in English Teaching*, Brighton; Falmer Press, pp. 229–33.

15 Quoted in Purves (1972).

5 Stop, look and listen

Previous chapters have looked at the situations and strategies which can facilitate or inhibit the development, in different aspects of English, of the child as thinker. In this chapter I want to emphasize and elaborate on three aspects implicit in much of what has gone before. The first (and briefest) section raises again the question of the English teacher's role and builds on earlier references to 'fixing', or engineering, contexts in which the desired mental operations can take place; the second section picks up on the centrality of perception as already described, particularly in Chapter 3, but pushes further the notion of parallels between English and Art; the third section – particularly relevant perhaps in the light of the recognition this has had in the second part of the Cox Report (1989) – is devoted to strategies for encouraging pupils in listening and, building especially on the references to Donald Graves (1983) as well as on the first section of this chapter, to ways in which the teachers can refine and improve their own listening.

Stopping: an invitation to teachers to do less teaching

Stopping is undervalued. There are too many teachers talking, too many pupils 'listening': there's too much teaching going on. The old road-safety slogan above was discontinued after it was found that children learnt it all right but used it not as a guide for action, but as an 'incantation', designed perhaps to ward off evil traffic. Other incantations may be placatory – pacifying the teacher or the system – avoiding confrontation, certainly, but also thought. Too much learning in school may be of these kinds.

Yet 'STOP' in the old slogan was meant to be purposive – a precondition for the efficacy of subsequent action. Used in this sense it recalls the old arguments about freedom – freedom *from* or freedom *for*. We might therefore begin by stopping just some of the noise, both external and internal, that can impede thought, in order to give a chance to productive silence. It is no coincidence that writers such as Marjorie Hourd (1949), Ted Hughes (1967) and James Moffett

(1968) have in various ways sought to emphasize reverie, silent concentration, even meditation. One wonders too what might happen if the relaxation exercises often employed in drama were a regular feature of English classes.

Then again there is what might be called 'experimental stopping'. What would happen, for example, if young children in primary schools for whom sitting still (or moving decorously around the room) is the normal and intolerable state, could stop and go for a jog round the playground, say every twenty minutes? What would happen if English teachers stopped marking so much, stopped thinking so pedagogically, and trusted intuition? What would happen if English rooms stopped being classrooms and became meeting places instead?

Like Shaw, Coleridge saw teaching as an 'unsatisfactory profession':

> Do not they all [he asked] possess a sort of mental odour? Are not all masters, all those who are held in estimation, not scholars but always masters, even in their sports; and are not the female teachers always teaching and setting right? Whilst both not only lose the freshness of youth, both of mind and body, but seem as though they never had been young. They who have to teach, can never afford to learn; hence their improgression.[1]

Coleridge's stance was, however, more interesting and more balanced than Shaw's. Coleridge saw teaching as 'a duty which if ably discharged is the highest and most important which society imposes'. And he also suggested that society was in some way responsible for – and should do something about – the apparently inevitable process which led to the loss of freshness and humanity. Partly, he implied, it was a matter of selection. Teachers appeared to fall into two categories – 'uncongenial' or 'unsound'. The uncongenial were not merely mentally odoriferous, they also possessed

> a subdued sobriety of disposition, the result of a process compared to which the course of a horse in a mill is positive enjoyment.

This he saw as reflecting what society both *did to them* and *wanted them to be like*.

His description of the other category interestingly anticipates the notion of good teaching as being in some ways subversive, since

> if they possess that buoyancy of spirit, which best fits them for communicating to those under their charge the knowledge it is held useful for them to acquire, they are deemed unsound.

During my own schooling, I was fortunate to meet at least one teacher who was in Coleridge's terms thoroughly 'unsound'. Lyons Wilson, who taught me art, gave me my first in-school experience of *really looking*. As well as normal art lessons, he held an appreciation class on Saturday mornings when he talked about pictures projected on to a screen with the aid of some kind of antique epidiascope. His basic unsoundness was never in doubt but was proved in particular by

1 his 'buoyancy of spirit': I can still recall the enjoyment which he conveyed as he drew our attention to weird details in Breughel's paintings

2 his evident interest in our reactions and comments
3 his irreverent and indiscreet comments on boys, members of staff and public schools in general
4 his interest in yoga and his ability, from a position alongside the lecturer's bench (behind which ar.y normal uncongenial teacher would have sat) to do a slowly controlled handstand on the bench itself.

He did not seem to do it to impress us – though this curious skill did much to raise the status of art in our eyes – but more as an expression of a *joie de vivre* uncommon in our experience of schoolmasters, and as indicating perhaps also a contempt for 'subdued sobriety'. For obvious reasons – what might nowadays be called a damage-limitation strategy – my school employed him only part-time.

Looking: some parallels between thinking processes in English and Art

Generally when someone is said to have been marked for life, this relates to a distressing or traumatic experience. For me, in one instance at any rate, it was not like that – some part of being taught by, or what I learned from, Lyons Wilson has remained with me, intuitively perceived as important. I do not know whether I was conscious of this when I first started teaching in a reasonably academic grammar school. All I know is that, as I tried to teach very intelligent and competent pupils, I felt that the problems they were encountering had much more to do with their way of looking at, remembering, thinking about, and imagining things than with technical and stylistic defects. I wrestled with the plain fact that, while I liked and respected them, their work bored me. And I suspected they felt the same.

Many teachers hit on good ideas not only out of instinct and intuition but also through frustration. Thus having tried with marginal success the best parts of the textbooks I was expected to use, I sought ways of supplementing this material; pictures seemed a promising resource. It was a small, pragmatic and hesitant beginning as I tried to relate some techniques of photography and painting to those employed by writers.[2] Though my confidence has grown since then, that early experience convinced me that the best pictures are your own collection, however ill-mounted, dog-eared and assembled from whatever unlikely sources. Perhaps the crucial factor about it is its disarming *un*packaging.

Certainly the remarkable thing about the paintings which Lyons Wilson brought in on those Saturday mornings was that they were *his*. Moreover he was wise enough not to expect us to admire them, learn about them or from them. He wanted to share them and to see what happened.

This is in sobering contrast to my own early efforts to use 'visual aids'. Under normal (i.e. pedagogic) circumstances, what one brings into a classroom – be it plasticine, poems, newspapers, or pictures – is not a gift. The teacher who rushes into a class on Monday morning doesn't 'just happen to have it with him' and the cynical old hands are correct in their initial reaction – 'Where's the catch?' A picture thus entering the classroom becomes quite unlike a picture in any other setting. Classrooms are places where things are not merely not what they seem to be but where things have a hard time *being* at all. It's not our fault entirely: we are fighting against the child's perception of the difference between school knowledge and 'real' knowledge.

A friend tells of a panic in his school, of frantic activity in the resources centre to get papers run off in time for a geography exam. Against all the odds, they succeeded, or so it seemed till someone discovered that the question on filling in names of cities had a map of Europe attached to it instead of one of North America. Too late. The exam went ahead. The pupils left the hall talking about the stupidity of it all. They had noticed the mistake over the map. But they had complied with the instructions all the same!

Had they lived a hundred years or so earlier those pupils might have taken part in the Charge of the Light Brigade, but the kind of learning implied by that tale is one that you cannot blame the individual teacher for. Unreality will eventually creep into school curricula, routines and teaching but it *need not have unchallenged sway*. As far as the use of visual material is concerned, resisting unreality involves (amongst other things) re-thinking the notion of stimulus as something applied from the outside. Such a concept leads to 'progressive' teaching which is not significantly different in the pupils' eyes from performance of a much more traditional kind: it's just a new way of pulling the puppets' strings. After only minimal training, most pupils can recognize a stimulus when they see one, even though the teacher says it's a poem.

When one of the first significant school texts of what may loosely be termed the stimulus-book type appeared, its title, *Reflections*,[3] was intended not merely to say something about its contents but was meant to indicate an underlying purpose; an invitation to particular kinds of intellectual activity. The contents were varied, interesting, relevant. By 'relevant' I mean that they were chosen by teachers skilled in building bridges between school reality and pupil (real-life) reality. The connection was potentially there, but relevance is not a quality wholly inherent in particular subject matter; it derives equally from the teaching context in which it is introduced. Depending on that setting, the hidden agenda is more or less intrusive and – what is important for our purposes – inhibits to a corresponding degree the kinds of thinking that can take place.

I referred in Chapter 3 to Michael Benton's *The First Two Rs*,[4] where he criticized the emphasis on stimulus material, the demand for responses at all costs, as a new kind of gradgrindery and suggested a different model for children's creative writing based largely on the composition process as described by practising writers. Before this Rosen and Rosen (1973: 145) had made the valuable point that in the private writing activity the child is involved not merely in 'responding to experience' (whether individual or supplied and engineered by the teacher) but in 'responding *to his responses*'. Robert Witkin in *The Intelligence of*

Feeling (1974: 24) follows a similar line in talking about 'sensing our sensing'. Stimuli are only really effective when they help to promote such responses and this occurs when the external object makes connections with what is inside the pupil's head. Such a happy outcome, moreover, is as much the result of the thinking climate of the classroom and of the strategies of the teacher as of any magic property in the stimulus itself.

As long as teachers see themselves as expert – as being there to teach – they will probably succeed in transforming the picture into a text or even, if they are old hands, into a *mystery*. As a consequence the kinds of thinking, imaginative and feeling response open to pupils remain very limited. The teacher may not realize what is happening: how the very fact that the picture on page 17, which the class has been told to look at, is in a book and the notion that teachers are people who 'know about books' ensure that pupils see pictures as things to be known about and hence natural feelings of interest, puzzlement, or antipathy are thereby rendered – in the child's mind – inadmissible. Of course some mysteries may be easy to penetrate; the demands being made on the pupils introduced to a picture of an old man are relatively clear if they have been doing a six-week unit on 'old age'. The mystery that is really useful, however, is the unsolved case in which teacher and class together look for and exchange solutions – in other words, the best kind of mystery is the one which intrigues.

If pictures are to be of any value, they have to stir the mind, and the mind has to be free to be so stirred, which will not happen if notions of acceptable response interpose between the picture and viewer any more than between story and listener.

It may not always be the teacher who gets in the way, however. Some early attempts to provide suitable 'sets' of visual material did this on their own. Often these were produced by people who had used pictures successfully in their own classrooms but who – perhaps under pressure from publishers anxious to produce 'teacher-proof' materials – were induced to add 'suggestions'. The simple fact that picture-cards were numbered, often in sets of thirty-six, might well have prompted the child who had received number one to wonder if that meant that there were still another thirty-five to go: hardly a stimulating reflection. The 'suggestions' constituted a much more serious interference however. One rather interesting picture had on the reverse side the following text.

> This old couple are standing, very bewildered, on a dockside in the United States. They are Hungarian and have never left their native land before. Their son, who emigrated to America some years before, has sent for them and now they are looking anxiously around for him. They do not speak a word of English and their hearts will be full of dread until they see the familiar face of their son and know they are safe.
>
> Try to imagine what the next few hours would be like for the couple in the picture if their son were delayed in coming to meet them and could not get a message to them. What difficulties would they have, in a land where nobody speaks Hungarian and they cannot read the simplest notice? Write a story or play about it.

By way of contrast with this admittedly extreme example of how not to stimulate by pictures, we may look at the reproduction of a 'story-board' in Figure 3. It suffers through reduction in size (original 11″ × 14″) and the loss of colour, but should be sufficient to give an idea of a totally different approach. Originally designed for use in the USA at kindergarten and first grade levels,[5] this material was an attempt to answer the question 'How do we break the silence barrier of some children who don't seem to attend to instruction?'

Figure 3

In the *Teachers' Guide* by Olivia W. Hill, there is a concise outline of the thinking behind the series and the general conclusions from field-testing together with examples of sample lessons and follow-up activities. This is impossible to précis and largely outside my scope but the first general conclusion from the field-testing is very interesting: 'the greatest value of the story-boards is their suggestibility. A higher level of thinking is involved in interpreting a story-board than in identifying the components in a realistic picture'.

In other words, this visual stimulus has an unusual quality: '*built-in ambiguity*'. In early work on visual material, a degree of ambiguity may well be an important agent in freeing response, and avoiding a search for right answers or production to order.

Initially all responses are interesting and are valid; such an accepting attitude is not flabbiness, but derives from a clear sense of purpose. It is crucial for us first to legitimize mental reflections of whatever sort, to sanction mental play, however aberrant, before we can begin to refine them. We begin with the acceptance and sharing of reactions, emphasizing *the interest that lies in the variety of the ways the mind works*. We want the learner's mind to attend to things intrinsically.

While much of this depends on factors in the classroom that have already been mentioned, another precondition of response to the inherent qualities of visual material has received less notice, and is more specific. It is not enough to look at things in order for the mind, as it were, to move on. We have to generate an interest in *the looking-act itself.* (An exactly parallel case may be made for concentration upon the listening act – the main thing many children learn in school about listening is when not to or when half-listening will suffice.) If one follows a child around a zoo or aquarium until something really catches his or her attention, or when one watches children under the spell of a really good story-teller, one has some idea of the quality of attention children are capable of and which is too rarely seen in school.

Our task therefore is to energize perception by exercising it – on as wide a range of material, and in as many situations as we can devise. A single example must suffice: to have a picture hanging up in front of a class may (though of course need not) lead to teacher exposition very little different from waving a poem in front of them and talking about it. On the other hand, to show a picture for a very short period (say two seconds), question the class about it, and then re-show it, perhaps for a longer period, is capable of arousing a much more strenuous visual attentiveness (in this connection slides have many advantages).

That is not all that is gained. Experiments have suggested that children tend to talk more freely when a picture is shown and then removed than when it is left in front of them.[6] The reason is not far to seek. The picture that is left in front of the child remains a text, something about which one can be proved wrong, where one can be blamed for 'missing something'. If the picture is removed, however, the image is left free to work in the pupil's mind. Thereafter, provided the teacher's stance is an open one, actively encouraging diversity of response, the pupil is able to respond in a variety of ways. Much interesting work is subsequently possible, listing and comparing such responses and tracing them back.

Such openness is less common than it should be simply because teachers remain obsessed with teaching, which is understandable given the anxiety produced by the pressures currently being put on them. In terms of visual material this has often meant that they have treated it as literature (which is fine) and expect the same constricted range of responses that literary works tra- ditionally elicit within a classroom (which is not). In dealing with film material they often tend to favour (or actually permit) only a few response strategies, pushing exclusively towards the narrational, explanatory or judgemental. (Even this range of options may be reduced according to their view of the class's ability.)

To ask a class what they thought of a film – for 'critical opinions' – is to leave out a whole range of intermediate mental processes upon which ultimately opinion might be based. This is the more serious in that film material tends to be more commonly used with students who are less good with words and who have a corresponding greater need of incubatory, tentative and exploratory response. What is needed is a type of questioning which first, *takes the pupil back into the experience of the film*, and second, *demands an initial answer which poses no difficulty in formulation*. What I have in mind is such a question as 'Thinking back over the film, which image(s) or single shot(s) is/are most clear in your memory?' Memories thus evoked are then available for discussion and comparison, into which the students will enter the more readily because they have been able to meet the teacher's first demand.

When we use visual material with a potentially strong emotional impact – or more to the point, which moves *us* – we have to guard against another danger, that of children pretending to empathize, because empathy is what teacher wants, and what teacher wants can get in the way of individual reflective response by interposing between the material and the student responding to it a whole set of inhibiting considerations. Given these dangers, the need is for an oblique approach. This will involve

1 Variety in teaching procedures (the introduction of a picture must not inevitably lead in one direction).
2 Allowing the meaning of a picture to be defined by the pupils, forcing them to speculate.
3 Asking questions of a kind which facilitates this and which, if effective, will elicit response but not force it. Stimulated feeling can all too easily degenerate into simulated feeling.

A favourite painting of mine is Degas's 'Absinthe Drinkers', where a man and a woman are shown seated at the same marble-topped table in a French café. The notion that though physically fairly close together they are mentally apart is conveyed mostly by the divergent directions of their gaze, the woman's eyes looking with sad reflectiveness towards the floor, the man morosely contemplating something perhaps outside the café window. Degas manages to leave unclear whether either of them is really looking at anything or whether, to modify the coy caption of a Victorian painting I knew well in my youth, their 'eyes are with [their] thoughts and they are far away'. If I like this painting particularly it is because it poses graphically the need to interpret or explain: questions like 'What's going on?' 'Who are they?' rise unbidden in the mind of whoever really looks at the picture. Like the story-card, it is full of teasing ambiguities.

Teachers may usefully encourage this reflective process. Forcing speculation, they may ask such questions as:

1 Why did the painter notice this scene in the first place?
2 Imagine the painter just outside the frame of the picture – tell me anything you can about him. What kind of pictures would he NOT paint? Why?

3 This painting is a kind of statement: in pairs list a few things you think (a) it is about, (b) it is not about.
4 Look at the painting a second time and try to find something you didn't notice at first. Can you explain why you didn't?
5 What effect is the painter trying to produce in your mind?
6 Write a single line of dialogue to go with this picture.

Questions like this help students to look at pictures without being too inhibited by the consciousness of their own ignorance; not only is their interest in pictures thus enhanced but also their attitude to the very act of looking is made more thoughtful and more positive. This may invigorate other kinds of perception and memory when they are directed to explore their own experience. More than this, the interested teacher may be able to establish parallels between the art of the painter and that of the poet, which lead to much more sensitive reflection about and response to poetry.

The idea of parallels is one which has grown on me since 1983: I suppose some such conception must have lain in the mind of whoever decided, a good number of years ago, that the Chief Examiner for the Postgraduate Certificate in Education in Art at Birmingham Polytechnic should be someone from a different field. It is the only post I have ever acquired on the novel basis of *interested ignorance*: equally surprising was the discovery of how much learning such a post might involve.

Learning situations often seem to reveal an inverse relationship between openness and expertise. To take an example, at Exeter I teach two PGCE groups for English – the 'main' group are English graduates, the 'subsids' are not. From the outset the 'subsids' are willing to suspend disbelief, to come to meet you, to *play*. 'Main' students normally take four or five weeks to reach the same position. And of course the effects are reciprocal: their anxiety may constrain me.

Expertise may be a burden; if one has defined and learnt to value oneself through a particular study or set of skills, one's stake in the matter makes for vulnerability. 'Real' experts know how much remains unknown; lesser mortals just carry around with them a guilt list – ever growing – of great books still not read. If you wish to try out the threat that another expert may pose, you might open a new group's first session with a remark like 'Well I expect you'll all be familiar with Bruner's *Studies in Cognitive Growth*', and watch for the reactions! Such vulnerability, by the way, is a fairly constant characteristic of the 'gifted' children who come to Kilve and shows itself in defensive anxiety when they are asked to do new or 'silly' things.

I offer this apparent digression primarily as another concrete example of the way situations determine the extent to which mental play and exploration is possible, and this is in many respects the same problem for teachers of English and Art. Second, it goes some way to explain why my contact with PGCE art students was so interesting. I met them in three major contexts:

1 *Workshops on the relation between language and art*
These focused not on the language of art but on the relevance of recent work on classroom language: teachers' language strategies, group talk, etc. A second thread sought to tie together or at least speculate about the relevance of my own work to the art room.

2 *Teaching practice*
Here I may have had more credibility, but the exchanges would have been incomplete without the third context.

3 *End of course exhibitions*
These are traditional in perhaps the majority of art courses; PGCE students have to display two kinds of work:
(a) That which reflects their own professional learning – the extension of their own artistic repertoire. Many have relatively specialized backgrounds – for example, jewellery or textiles – which leaves them with a fairly restricted armoury for the classroom. Some of their deepest satisfactions were gained from extended workshop experience in which they had had the opportunity to try, and acquire, new skills.
(b) The second kind of work displayed was that of children taught on teaching practice. Generally the student-teachers had started from areas where they were most confident (or felt best equipped). Generally, too – and this was directly a result of their workshop experiences in new media – their displays showed a progressive willingness to take risks. In my own experience some of the best teaching comes when one is working at the fringes of what one 'knows'.

Through these three kinds of contact the parallels between English and Art were clarified and extended. In the exhibition situation a sample of students had the opportunity to show and talk me through their work at some length. Here particularly my lack of expertise seemed an asset: they were free to talk about successes, failures and experiments with scarcely a trace of the defensiveness that external examiners learn to expect. My main impression was of their interest and genuine desire to share such experiences.

On this basis, and with proper diffidence, I should like to suggest, first, some relatively obvious parallels, and then some areas of rather more complex overlap.

Parallels

Looking

It may seem unnecessary to suggest that this is an important aspect of both subjects (which is of course not to imply any joint monopoly); English and Art need to explore ways of making looking both more strenuous and more interesting. To achieve this, 'effort' is not as necessary as the encouragement of consistent attentiveness.

Classroom climate

Everything that has been said about this applies equally to the art room though it has particular advantages. First, it is a place where a certain amount of physical movement is taken as natural. Second, it offers, often unlike the English room, the opportunity of talking while doing.

Common problems

The most common of these is quite simple: enabling children to explore the medium. I have referred at some length to problems in English that have to do with 'neatness' and presentation. An almost exact parallel can be found in Art. This may be manifested in a very cramped use of the medium, whether pencil, paint, crayon or whatever; or in a nervous tendency to tear up half of one's work because it falls short of some imaginary standard:

> In the school study one of the problems raised had been to do with what line the staff should take in order to help the quiet over-introverted child who seems to have insufficient contact with the external world. It was through study of the experience of the free drawings that I came to understand more about the kind of problem that the over-introverted child is struggling with; and also, incidentally, what the over-extroverted child is running away from.

> (Milner 1971: xviii)

Overlaps

Representing or symbolizing

This heading is a somewhat crude shorthand for a dimension of choice that is often very complicated. I referred above to the tearing-up phenomenon which derives from some imaginary standard. That standard, however, is often closely related to notions of some kind of representational adequacy or correctness. Again, Marion Milner throws light on this: speaking of adults and children whose capacity to produce ideas was inhibited, she writes

> It was clear that these patients had an extremely idealised notion of what their products ought to be, and the task of objective evaluation of what they in fact produced appeared to be so disillusioning to them that they often gave up the attempt to produce anything.

> (Milner 1971: 149)

Both English and Art teachers need to combat this by encouraging children to 'lash around a bit', whether in paint or words. However we may manage it, our aim is to sanction experiment, to encourage the making of an enjoyable mess. I think there is a connection here with George Sampson's (1921) idea of encouraging fluency (see Chapter 3).

Marion Milner's work, which resembles in general viewpoint that of Marjorie Hourd, enables us to push further the notion of climate already discussed and to understand more clearly the way clinical insights may help us to understand the way the right climate can encourage the greater range of thinking strategies that we are seeking. Arguing the case for 'absent-mindedness', she asserts

> it is a pity that the expressive word 'reverie' has been so largely dropped from the language of psycho-pathology, and the overworked word phantasy made to carry such a heavy burden of meaning. For the word 'reverie' does emphasise the aspect of absent-mindedness, and therefore brings in what I feel to be a very important aspect of the problem, that is, the necessity for a certain quality of protectiveness in the environment. For there are obviously many circumstances in which it is not safe to be absent-minded; it needs a setting, both physical and mental. It requires a physical setting in which we are freed, for the time being, from the need for immediate practical expedient action; and it requires a mental setting, an attitude, both in the people around and in oneself, a tolerance of something which may at moments look very like madness.
>
> (Milner 1971: 163–4)

These quotations come in the last part of her book, where she tries to give a rationale for insights gained in the course of her own painting but based on the evidence of sustained self-observation. In a sense her book charts a journey which is partly characterized by a move away from the representational towards responses that are not merely more subjective but more symbolic in mode. The move involves a letting-go which from the outset is quite clearly perceived as a risky business:

> Certainly it seemed that as long as one is content to live amongst the accepted realities of the common sense world, the fear of losing one's hold on the solid earth may remain unrecognised; but that as soon as one tries to use one's imagination, to see with the inner as well as with the outer eye, then it may have to be faced.
>
> (Milner 1971: 25)

Later, reflecting on Santayana's essay 'The suppressed madness of sane men' she comes to a conclusion very close to theoretical studies of the reading experience which have begun to exert some influence even at classroom level:

> Thus the substance of experience is what we bring to what we see, without our own contribution we see nothing. But I wanted to add that of course imagination itself does not spring from nothing, it is what we have made within us out of all past relationships with what is outside, whether they were realised as outside relationships or not.
>
> (Milner 1971: 27–8)

While such a line of thought is gaining wider acceptance, some aspects of Marion Milner's argument – partly because of her particular clinical standpoint – may appear purely esoteric; interesting perhaps but divorced from classroom reality. Before returning to earth, as it were, and attempting to find some mundane parallels to processes she is describing, we should perhaps look at her account of 'changes in the sense of self' that occurred in her move away from the representational towards a freer form.

In this book I have tried to describe how, under particular conditions of making the free drawings, something new, unexpected did in fact emerge. The phrase 'contemplative action' had seemed an appropriate description of the process: 'contemplative' to distinguish it from practical expedient action, 'action' to distinguish it from pure contemplation, to bring in the fact of the moving hand.

The essential thing about this contemplative mood, combined with action, was that it involved me in a giving up of the wish to make an exact reproduction of anything I had seen. Since obviously one cannot anyway produce a truly realistic copy of any object known in the external world, for marks on a two-dimensional surface can never be an exact reproduction of a three-dimensional object, it would seem that this was not a very difficult wish to give up. Nevertheless, in spite of my early discovery that no attempt to copy the appearance of objects was what my eye liked there was still a continual inner battle to be waged against the urge to attempt this mechanical copying; and this, in spite of years of experience of the fact that it was only when I had discarded this wish to copy that the resulting drawing or painting had any life in it, any of the sense of a living integrated structure existing in its own right.

(Milner 1971: 153–4)

Incubatory processes

I suggested earlier some reasons why Marjorie Hourd's insights had received less acceptance than those of some of her successors, her combination of literary and psychoanalytical insight posing some real difficulties. Rather similarly, Marion Milner relates insights from the world of art and poetry to her clinical experience. If we are concerned, however, with ways of seeing and reflecting, with developing strategies for thinking about and responding to the world about us, her writings may help to clarify our general approach and strengthen our core of belief. It is to be hoped that this understanding may inform our practice, especially where our effort is directed towards situations in which children may be helped to find out what they think through activities which facilitate the incubation of ideas.

To take an example from the last passage quoted, I would point to Milner's distinction between 'contemplative action' and 'practical expedient action' where she suggests the idea of 'the moving hand helping contemplation'. (This may link up with John Berger's idea that, for the average Englishman, the potting shed or workshop was the place where he could best engage in introspection.) I have increasingly believed that the artroom was potentially a rich environment for talk, precisely because exploratory talk could be sustained by doing, and vice versa.

An activity that might appropriately take place in either English or Art is collage.[7] From English teachers' point of view, the range of materials will be probably confined to the visual, such as old magazines and so on; they will also have to tolerate – in a classroom probably not designed for it – a good deal of mess, scissors, glue, piles of newspapers and Sunday supplements. Initially, the end products may appear disappointing but observation of the process may offer substantial encouragement: an atmosphere of increasing busyness and absorption; edgy adolescents apparently calmed (rather than moved to violence) by the physical manipulation of scissors. This quietening may be the prelude to an increasing exchange of ideas, an exchange which can be – is expected to be – desultory. Thus – as they continue to snip or rifle their way through magazines – ideas may come. In their own time. When pupils have become used to such an occasional activity as this, affording as it does opportunity for a kind of reverie, discussion may gradually become freer and even extend into such technical problems as emphasis, arrangement, juxtaposition and contrast. Though they may not be particularly articulate, we should not underestimate them. After all, they are used to taking in visual images and may well prove quite visually literate.

In this connection, it may seem strange that having talked about film and about pictures, I have made no explicit mention of television. One problem is clear from the outset: watching television is part of the child's private world and hence none of the teacher's business. Equally clearly, however, the emphasis placed on pictures, on adverts, on *really looking* can bear upon this private world; possibilities exist for the teacher to exploit the connections. To do so effectively calls for tact, delicacy and good relations with those taught. Invitations to children to watch particular programmes (which we may deem – at least potentially – educational) may be perceived as pedagogic trespass on their privacy.

The teachers who can best make connections are those who, first, are aware of what children normally watch and what they normally get out of their viewing and who, second, are subtle enough in their procedures to recognize the difference between incidental cross-referencing to television and poaching on the pupils' preserves. The best use of television is rarely full-frontal but rather oblique, curtailed in length and intended to establish common points of reference rather than to trawl the *TV Times* for lesson fodder. Some of the viewing that children themselves would see as intrinsically less important – news items or adverts for example – may provide safer ground than literary critiques of their favourite soaps and may yield fruitful opportunities for the imitation (or parodying) of linguistic models provided by television.

Other strategies for incubation suggest themselves as applicable to both English and Art: drawing, mime and tableaux, and film-making and film-scripting.

Drawing   The possibilities here are fairly obvious since the connections between drawing, talking and writing are often thoroughly established early on in the primary school. There may be difficulties later on. First, children often feel good at one activity and not at another; some of the gifted writers at Kilve also felt there was something *infra dig.* about being asked to draw. Part of the trouble seems to be a too narrow conception of thinking handed on by their teachers and partly the anxiety engendered by experimenting with things that one 'is not good at'. The second major difficulty is less serious and rather more fun to combat: this is the development at secondary level of a mentality that used to be shown, in the days which union members now probably remember with nostalgia, in what were called demarcation disputes. In the classroom this shows itself in a feeling that an *English* teacher has no business to be messing around with *Art*. At a higher level drawing and indeed 'doodling' have been found to have a place. Here again the process can be said to be partly incubatory, partly the production of what Witkin (1974: 180) calls a 'holding-form' which makes possible a further stage of mental exploration.

In an article 'The mind's eye' Geoff Fox and Brian Merrick explained the origins and the rationale behind the use of visual responses to literature in work with B.Ed. students.[8] They began by giving a particularly engaging restatement of the pragmatic approach to which I referred in the introduction:

> One of the characteristics of our collaborative teaching is a kind of cheerful blundering about in pursuit of what seems like a good idea at the time. We tend to encourage each other in this, trusting this way forward rather than the neatly pre-packed course which can so inhibit team-teaching. Our attempts to foster students' visual responses to literary texts began in this tentative manner. We started from the fairly safe premise that one of the liveliest sources of pleasure for the engaged reader of fiction and poetry was an ability to create pictures in the mind's eye. It is another safe step to recognise that the nature of these pictures is in part determined by what a text offers and in part by the ways in which each reader characteristically visualises a text. In a series of interviews with younger secondary age children, we tried to explore how different individuals brought to mental life the images they derived from the same extract from a novel. Whenever we have tried to find out just what goes on inside readers' heads, the most obvious (but endlessly fascinating) recognition is the highly idiosyncratic quality of each response. In this investigation, some readers superimposed their own experiences upon the extract almost to the exclusion of the text; others had clear, neatly arranged, representational pictures; others had a more abstract impression of the scene described.
>
> We noted in passing that the children we interviewed palpably enjoyed telling us what they could see with their inner eyes; often they told us so spontaneously. They liked being the dominant partner in a long conversation with an attentive adult, of course; each child had unique evidence which only she or he could give, and we clearly wanted to hear it. Beyond that, however, was a lively pleasure in dwelling upon the picture in the mind's eye: filling out some detail, perhaps, or modifying the picture as they talked. Some of their pleasure, in short, lay in the development and refinement of their responses, which seemed to us to have clear implications for our own classroom practice.

'This crude exploration of the pictures in readers' heads posed several questions', which the article goes on to consider in detail, especially these points: first, what might we do to encourage and develop this aspect of literary response? Second, are pictures in the mind's eye best left there undisturbed?

Mime and tableaux   I do not want here to argue the case for teaching mime or its relationship with writing; merely to assert that it calls on and develops qualities of concentration and visualization that appear valuable in both Art and English. A very early collaboration with a colleague led to his using mime in pottery classes. Equally it seems to me to offer new opportunities and dimensions to figure drawing. Tableau work, where groups of figures are moulded by a 'sculptor' to convey an abstract idea, or – in a series – to tell a story, seems an equally rich area for experiment.

Film-making and 'film-scripting'   Again these are activities that could feed into either subject, and offer frameworks for new ways of thinking and perceiving. (In English lessons I have seen film-scripting exercises offering firm support to children who were seeking to tell a story visually but lacked the skill or confidence to use a normal narrative form.)

Where looking leads
Though this has been touched on already, the purpose here is to explore what looking at things can do to our thinking, and to connect this with ideas about incubation. In an average English or Art lesson, if you ask children to look *hard* at an object, they will anticipate a subsequent task, that is they will have to draw it or write about it. Such foreknowledge does little to liberate their thinking. For the student of English the anticipated task may well be 'description', the difficulties of which have already been indicated.

During most of the courses at Kilve we have paid particular attention to this problem, and the very high staff–student ratio, together with the natural co-operativeness of the students, has enabled us to try things that would have otherwise seemed impossible. For example, on several courses students have been instructed to leave the house, go out into the grounds, look around, gradually focus on some small detail that caught their eye and concentrate on it for several minutes. They were further instructed not to worry about it but quite specifically to try to relax (go quiet, listen to their breathing, etc.) while keeping their attention focused on the chosen object. Thus on one frosty morning I had the almost unnerving experience of watching about fifty 12-year-olds spread out over the delightful grounds clad in hoar-frost, standing motionless. Looking at things. They had been instructed to maintain total silence from the time they left the lecture room until they had returned and had completed notes both on what they had looked at and any feelings thus evoked. And they did as they were told!

The exercise was part of a concentrated drive to free them from notions about acceptable writing and to regain a proper interest in the act of looking itself. One of the questions at the end of the course took the form 'Has anything we've done helped you?' Clearly such a question is dangerous – a bit like asking them to tell us how marvellous we were. It seemed worth asking, however, because the level of trust and interest generated in a week when most children were working for about nine hours a day, often in one-to-one contact with students, made the obvious risks acceptable.

Reassuringly, replies were neither uniform nor uniformly favourable.

'No,' answered one hard case.

'I'm not sure but I think I'm a bit better at rounders!' answered another, though she added more encouragingly, 'The drama was helpful because I've got confidence in making a right fool of myself in front of everyone.'

Others reflected the hard case viewpoint more compassionately:

'I haven't really found anything helpful. Sorry!!'

'No. But the football will come in handy!'

Another felt this perhaps even more strongly:

'I have learnt to play football on this course (I'm a girl).'

Our own observation of the children on this exercise out of doors strongly suggested that *most*, at some level or other, had been intrigued or interested. It was good, however, to have several responses which implied this, while thirteen made specific reference to it. Here are just a few:

I have found going outside and choosing an object (for yourself) and writing notes about it helpful. When you write it out you can really use your imagination.

One thing that I have done that I found helpful is going out for ideas not just staying in and thinking because you usually come up with an idea you have already used.

I found it helpful to go outside and look at a particular object and define what I thought about it.

I found that going outside to examine things was helpful as I could see things I had not seen before . . . hopefully it will make my work more interesting.

The Kilve experience I suppose is a bit like a brief spell in what used to be called a laboratory school. But experiments can take place in laboratories and such experience can strengthen both insight and conviction. Problems of re-applying such insights remain, as one realist reminded us (though I'm not sanguine about his proposed solution to the problem):

I have learned different ways of doing things, but all the work in school is so different to what we do here it will be of little use what-so-ever, but if we tell our teacher some of the things it will be very useful.

For some of these children, looking at things closely and describing with an accuracy unfettered by preconceptions about 'good words' will be the main gain. For many others a closer approach to some kind of photographic accuracy will be the best we can hope for; it will have derived from a better quality of attention and have led to the more effective use of words.

All this is consonant with the first emphasis Ted Hughes (1967) placed on 'telling things the way they are'. In the remarkable 'recipe' (quoted in full in Chapter 3) he suggested a second phase of development towards the symbolic, yet rooted in his clear perception of where children are and, even more remarkably, expressing a formula that may render a very complex process comprehensible to them.

> The descriptions will be detailed, scientific in their objectivity and microscopic attentiveness.
> After some exercises of this sort, the pupil should be encouraged to extend the associations out from the object in every direction, as widely as possible, keeping the chosen object as the centre and anchor of all his statements.
> Once the pupil has grasped the possible electrical connections between the objective reality and some words of his, this exercise, which at first might seem dull enough, becomes absorbingly exciting. Even where it produces poor results, the effort towards this kind of perception and description affects the way the pupil looks at, and attends to, everything.
> Where this type of exercise can be pursued intensively, the same object should be tackled repeatedly, four or five times, on different days.
>
> (Hughes 1967: 64)

Though the instructions are simple, the clear intention is to set up a routine which is in fact rigorous both in the initial intensive 'photographic' stage and the subsequent one. Whether teachers feel capable of following the demanding routine suggested in the last paragraph will depend on the degree of their conviction. But there is no doubt in my mind that, as Hughes suggests, repetition will show results.

The particular point to emphasize at this stage is the move away from the representational towards, if not the symbolic, at least the subjective response. The extraordinarily simple and effective teaching point here is the idea of '*keeping the chosen object as the centre and anchor of all statements*'.

You may look, for example, at a broken doll lying in long grass at the end of a neglected garden. In the first stage you merely describe it; later you may look at it, interspersing elements of description with thoughts that occur to you as you continue looking: in this you are using the doll almost like a set of notes which, however, leave you feeling safe enough to venture on the occasional digression. Instead of repelling thoughts like boarders you let them in. A final stage may be where, *through looking at the doll*, you find yourself writing about nostalgia, or lost childhood.

For those children (and indeed, in my experience, teachers) who manage to approach such a way of responding, it will not merely lead to a wider range of thinking and feeling but also to a deeper enjoyment of the medium itself. Rosen and Rosen's (1973) idea of 'responding to their responses' or Witkin's (1974) 'sensing their senses' will be apparent in very much the same way, as Marion Milner has indicated:

> what the painter does conceptualise in non-verbal symbols is the astounding experience of how it feels to be alive, the experience known from inside, of being a moving, living body in space, with capacities to relate oneself to other objects in

space. And included in this experience of being alive is the very experiencing of the creative process itself.

(Milner 1971: 159)

I have not attempted here to draw parallels with work in Art, partly because of my own lack of experience, partly because I trust the Art teachers who have followed the argument thus far to find their own.

Use of 'realized form'

Some of the dangers of the ways a teacher may 'offer' to a class a painting, poem or piece of music have already been made clear, especially where such an offering is intended to elicit admiration or lead to either analysis or instant ('stimulated') response. Experience of examining the work done with children by Art students suggests that they may often have a better instinct for using 'realized forms' to stimulate not merely imitation but also playful experiment. I recall many exhibitions of work where, for example, a few reproductions of, say, Picasso or Van Gogh are set against much pupils' work, which the originals – through the mediation of the teacher – have in the proper sense liberated. The crux would seem to be not the handing over of a Van Gogh recipe (although some cooking instructions may well be appropriate) but of helping the children to see things in different ways.

One reason why the use of models is approached more timidly by English teachers – apart from the fatuous notion that imitation is cramping or wrong – has to do with their relation to their subject. Art teachers have got where they are through a great deal of creative activity and some analysis; English teachers' experience sadly has usually been the precise opposite. It is hard for them therefore to convey the practitioner's enthusiasm for painting with one's big toe, or chunking paint with a palette knife!

Real pictures of course are not there just to be imitated, nor to stimulate; like literature they need to be part of an environment in which they exist to be 'read'. In a passage which interestingly parallels that by Empson (quoted in Chapter 4, p. 70), Roger Fry emphasizes the part played in aesthetic response by *recognition*:

> It may be objected that many things in nature, such as flowers, possess these two qualities of order and variety in a high degree, and these objects do undoubtedly stimulate and satisfy that clear disinterested contemplation which is characteristic of the aesthetic attitude. But in our reaction to a work of art there is something more – there is consciousness of purpose, the consciousness of a peculiar relation of sympathy with the man who made this thing in order to arouse precisely the sensations we experience. And when we come to the higher works of art, where sensations are so arranged that they arouse in us deep emotions, this feeling of a special tie with the man who expressed them becomes very strong. We feel that he has expressed something which was latent in us all the time, but which we never realised, that he has revealed us to ourselves in revealing himself. And this recognition of purpose is, I believe, an essential part of the aesthetic judgement proper.[9]

Listening

'Good boys and good girls always listen.
To learn, we must listen.
We must listen all the time.
Good boys and girls never talk,
but they always listen.
We should listen and listen and listen!'
To you teacher,
And your words, your words, your words.
Your words, your words, your words,
your words.

(Albert Cullum)[10]

And then a scholar said, Speak of Talking.
And he answered, saying:
You talk when you cease to be at peace with your thoughts;
And when you can no longer dwell in the solitude
of your heart you live in your lips, and sound is a
diversion and a pastime.
And in much of your talking, thinking is half
murdered.
For thought is a bird of space, that in a cage of words may
indeed unfold its wings but cannot fly.

(Kahlil Gibran)[11]

There are people old enough to know better who apparently take no trouble to
understand what is said to them. They have never learned to listen. To know when
not to listen is a valuable art in this world of bores; but the act should be under our
own control.

(Sampson 1921: 74)

According to Douglas Barnes and many others, one of the major things children
learn about listening is to recognize when it is not entirely necessary: their
increasing reliance on 'partial listening' may be seen as quite sensible adaptive
reaction to over-exposure. Once again George Sampson was ahead of his time:

There is far too much monologue in the teacher's school-work and far too much
passive listening in the child's; frequent exercises in co-operative listening are good
for both.

(Sampson 1921: 74)

Since Sampson's day, and especially in recent years, the literature devoted to this
problem has steadily increased: the evidence is now as extensive as it is
depressing.

What is perhaps not as generally recognized is that listening capacity seems to
decrease in direct proportion to the length of education received. The higher the
educational eminence which people achieve, the more attenuated their listening

capacity seems to become: in the case of some head teachers and professors this shows itself in an almost mystical imperviousness to outside verbal interference. (There appears, incidentally, to be some evidence of this phenomenon within the medical profession, where listening capacity may also be inversely proportional to status.) I would argue that there is a strong case for training in listening to provide specially for those members of the teaching profession who are – in the repellent jargon of the day – referred to as 'senior management'.

Conditions for listening

While children become inured to the amount of teacher-talk that washes over them and devise their own strategies for coping with it, there appear to be certain conditions in which they may actually listen to teacher:

1 *When the teacher ventures into ordinary converse*, perhaps involving personal anecdote or story-telling, as already suggested with reference to another Cullum poem (quoted in Chapter 2).
2 *When the teacher anticipates difficulties in listening:* the account of Clara's difficulties at a poetry reading (see Chapter 4) mirrors too closely for comfort the experience of many pupils being read to enthusiastically by teachers. I have known student teachers read as many as three very dense and taxing poems to a sixth form without intermission, discussion or even a text in front of them. Fortunately, however, there is a growing awareness of the difficulty of sustained high level academic listening and teachers make increasing provision to smooth (and vary) the listener's path.
3 *When the teacher makes listening a deliberate challenge*, in which case facing difficulty may become a productive game. I will return to this later when discussing strategies but it is interesting, particularly in the light of the Cox Report (1989), to reflect that in *1921* George Sampson made listening the third essential element in his English 'programme' and sought to make it interestingly demanding:

> Read a short simple poem to a class, even of older children, such a poem as 'Home they brought her warrior dead', and ask individual children to come out and repeat it to the others, either in the original words or their own, and you will be astonished to find, not merely how little they have remembered, but how little they have heard. Dictate to a seventh standard a short stanza – say, of *The Ancient Mariner* – and ask the boys to write it down after one hearing, and you will find that very few of them have really heard it. They have heard a few isolated words, but they have not heard the stanza as a whole thing. The limiting of dictation to a mere spelling test is a misuse of a valuable instrument. There should be a regular use of sense-dictation to give practice in the art of consecutive listening. Dictate a stanza, not phrase by phrase, but as a whole, and expect, not mere accuracy of spelling, but accuracy of apprehension. Dictate short prose passages – proverbs at first, then brief sentences, then longer sentences, and expect that the class should be able to reproduce, not

merely some of the words, but all of the meaning. You will be training them to do something really difficult and really valuable, namely, to listen consecutively and constructively.

(Sampson 1921: 72–3)

4   *Where teachers work hard to improve their own reading and story-telling.* As Benton and Fox argue

A teacher who cannot read aloud well is seriously handicapped. Reading aloud well is not essentially a matter of technique – a teacher's reading is an index of the kinds of confidence he has available to him and of his relationship with the class: a willingness to be experimental – playful, even – with his voice, to hold a pause, to characterize anyone from a goose to an archbishop. Ultimately, good reading grows from a sense of personal freedom and security whose discovery, and rediscovery, are at the heart of good teaching.

(Benton and Fox 1985: 111)

5   *Where the classroom climate is conducive to listening.* As the quotation above made clear, apart from reading technique, effective delivery depends also on the teacher's relationship with the class. I would add that listening depends on all the relationships within the class. Here strategies for group work – where the teacher gets out of the way – are crucial, for different kinds of group talk demand different kinds of listening. It is for this reason that I have for some years interviewed applicants for my PGCE main English course in *pairs*. At certain points in the proceedings they are called upon to interview each other as well as to co-operate in the presentation of one or two poems. This allows me the chance to hear how well they listen to *each* other (obviously in a one-to-one interview situation they will listen to me, assuming they want a place).

Some of the most interesting and recurrent responses of the children at Kilve to the question 'What have we done that has helped you?' related to group work. I believe this was precisely because it gave opportunities for listening – and for sharing – as well as for talking. In all, seventeen out of forty-nine mentioned group work as particularly helpful, for example:

The whole course has been a help, especially group work. I found that I especially liked working in groups on writing.

First you got us to speak freely and to get to know people. You included work in fun . . .

Here I felt that being in groups and all discussing things, and working on a few different things at once in a group, especially exhibiting work in different ways has helped me. . . . the fact that there is not such a tense school atmosphere . . . is very helpful . . .

I think I've learnt to work in a group and to take my turn.

This last short comment seems particularly significant. For many of these children the main source of self-valuing has been their success in reading and writing – both private activities. Given the new experience of working with children of similar ability, their normal modes of work could be modified and they found both a new confidence through talking and new interest in listening to their peers.

Strategies for listening

Whatever tactics are used the aim remains constant: to raise the level of interest in the listening act itself. Often, quite simply, to make it fun to listen. In this connection the strong emphasis in the Cox Report (1989) on 'active listening' is particularly welcome. George Sampson (1921) was particularly keen on exercises that promoted listening for meaning: 'training them to do something really difficult and really valuable, namely to listen consecutively and constructively'. I quoted some of his suggestions earlier and though some aspects of these may now seem dated, they form a useful starting-point.

I have used techniques like his with children of widely varying ability; short passages read for intensive listening practice and leading to various kinds of comprehension – factual, inferential and evaluative. Passages full of facts which listeners are called on to remember can lead to a quite enjoyable competitive game. With practice pupils can also reconstruct quite extended chunks of text, much as Sampson suggested.

The idea of such ideas being fun may become clearer through a particular tactic that may usefully be employed at the start of a campaign to 'pep up' listening. The teacher, early on in the lesson, reads a short poem or passage and immediately afterwards calmly asks the class (possibly working in pairs) *to write it down*. This should normally elicit the shouts of anguished protest on which the teacher was relying. With any luck, the second poem to be read – which should be simple enough to give them a chance – will be listened to in *a quite different way*. After such an exercise it is a good idea to explore the problems of listening in a general class discussion.

Though what follows offers further suggestions, as the Bullock Report (1975) noted, listening has to be seen as an aspect of a wider whole: its importance is indeed implicit in a range of activities already described in preceding chapters.

The inadequate provision of tape recorders in schools is a serious block to progress and may partially explain why teachers use them so rarely. It remains a great pity, however, that more do not set aside a few hours, perhaps at weekends, collecting their own store of listening material from as wide a range of sources as possible. A little homework done on the *Radio Times* can yield a very interesting mixed bag, enabling the teacher to come to class armed with a whole set of new voices. Very short extracts from plays or other dialogues can raise the listening temperature immediately and can energize thinking as a result. Given only two or three lines of dialogue, pupils can often draw shrewd inferences about the age, appearance and situation of the characters involved and often too make interesting predictions about the rest of the play. I could list a range of possibilities, but readers may well prefer to peruse their own *Radio Times* for themselves.

As far as the teacher is concerned, the other most obvious use of the tape recorder is for prepared readings; besides being good practice, especially for those who are diffident readers, it has other advantages. First, it avoids the dual task of controlling the class and reading interestingly at the same time. Second, it makes some pauses possible without breaking the rhythm, and enables the teacher to stand, for example, at the back of the class. Third, the teacher's voice on tape is different, and is differently attended to; children are also often grudgingly conscious of such efforts made on their behalf. Finally, it may reduce strain on the teacher's voice, particularly the probationer's.

On p. 27 I described children taping their own narratives, at an early age. Secondary school children are generally used to gadgetry and may, *because of this*, find things to tape which the teacher had never thought of. Initially the instructions for taping tasks may be made fairly simple, however, in order to build confidence in using the machine. A good starter is often a 'sound quiz', in which each group in the class has to record perhaps ten sounds, which the rest are then challenged to identify. This is not merely fun in class but the preparation of the tape itself demands strenuous (and imaginative) listening. In later stages, making 'sound-tracks' for particular purposes can lead to full-scale imitation or parody of various types of radio programmes, the latter exercise demanding really careful listening to and discussion of proposed models. In this kind of work the aim is that with increasing confidence and skill, groups of children should be encouraged to make their own choices for tape projects.

Clive Sutton's *Communicating in the Classroom* has a section on teaching 'Active Listening', which like the rest of the book has a number of practical suggestions. These are prefaced by some important general remarks, for example:

> Almost the only reliable indicator of better performance is that we tend to listen best when we have to take some action based upon what we have heard. This, however, is the key to helping pupils to be better learners of careful listening. They must have some reason for listening carefully.[12]

Later, after reference to levels of listening comprehension, as revealed by an American listening test, the author argued the need to consider the kinds of listening demanded by different situations and 'to build into lessons occasions when each is emphasised'. He went on to suggest four kinds, requiring ascending degrees of concentration. 'Casual listening' might occur with background music. 'Conversational listening' required more attention but little intellectual effort. 'Appreciative listening' involved 'undivided attention to a selected pattern of sounds'. The most intense concentration was however demanded by 'Critical listening', where the listening was essential to evaluation, whether of a car engine or of a music pupil.

This whole section of the book is interesting, as are the practical suggestions for activities which follow, for example:

> *Following instructions:* pupils draw a map or diagram entirely from oral instruction given by the teacher, or one of the class. Afterwards discuss how and why misunderstanding occurred. In another version of this pupils trace a route on a map entirely from oral instructions. (In science use a circuit diagram or a chart of blood vessels.)

> *Interference on the line:* use a tape recording such as those prepared by the Schools Council Oracy Project, where sections are deliberately omitted or obscured. Have the class infer what is in the missing section, with reasons. (Student teachers could prepare such a tape of a conversation about the topic currently being studied.)

> *Comparing notes:* use five to ten minutes from a recorded schools broadcast. Pupils take notes, and afterwards compare their perceptions of the main points.

Apart from such purposeful activities as these, others may have a stronger reflective or play element. Clearly in English there is a place – as suggested by Heaney's poem quoted in Chapter 1 – for some use of music, though only if the teacher likes music (as well as children) and is able to relate it flexibly to other aspects. Where this is so, however, the opportunity is opened up for a kind of reverie, especially where the listening is not always followed by a writing assignment (any such mechanical sequence being calculated to produce indifferent writing as well as constrained listening). Often music might be used in much the same way as suggested in the beginning of the article by Fox and Merrick quoted earlier to lead to a discussion perhaps of pictures in the head and to establish and accept the diversity of responses, including negative ones.

It seems quite appropriate to use such listening activities as an exploration, perhaps to enhance general understanding of what listening means or what happens to different people when they listen to music. This may not be too far removed from another activity which I would call listening in the head. This builds on the notion that the silent reading of poetry partly depends on 'hearing it'; one of the best comprehension questions on a poem is still for me, 'How should it be read?'

Finally, at the level of pure play I am reminded of various narrative games which involve a repetition that depends on listening. Thus in a game, original source unknown but called, I believe, 'Passing the Buck', the initial stage has a single person telling a (hopefully gripping) story in the middle of a ring of people. When this person has had enough or run out of inspiration, he or she hands over 'the buck' (any object will do if you don't happen to have a conch handy) to the person immediately in front, who then gets up, stands in front of someone else, *repeats the story thus far*, adds a further instalment, and then passes the buck to a third narrator, who therefore has to begin with a double-length recapitulation.

The listening teacher

> 'Good morning, class!
> Today I will prepare you for the future.
> Listen carefully,
> and don't interrupt!
> Are there any questions? . . .
> None?
> Good!'[13]

Normally Albert Cullum's poems speak through the child, but here – in perhaps the bitterest poem of his collection – he takes on the voice of the teacher. I began this section with something of the same criticism but I should not like to end on such a note – not least because I know that I have at some time or other been guilty of most offences I have cited (which is of course why I attack them with some fervour!).

I would like therefore to proceed towards a conclusion by offering some positive suggestions for the teacher. How can one help the teacher to listen better? Not, I believe, simply by offering recipes for more successful classroom management. We need to start from the position suggested in the introduction: low morale, low pay, inadequate funding, and the fairly asinine or at least simplistic panaceas offered by politicians. Given all this, where does better listening for teachers start? I would suggest not with children but amongst teachers themselves.

If you have ever listened in to conversations in staffrooms, one of the saddest impressions is the amount of defensiveness around. I can never forget the insights behind the humour of Edward Blishen's *Roaring Boys*: the picture of the supply teacher following in the steps of several others who had stood in front of the same diabolical class, quailed and fled; and especially in the interview with the headmaster who informed him that the important thing was 'to keep them under your thumb'. At this point in the proceedings he demonstrated with his own thumb, which to Blishen's anxious eyes was like 'a pocket cudgel'. This demonstration, far from being helpful, caused Blishen, looking covertly at his own thumb, to reflect upon its pathetic inadequacy for the task ahead.

Some teachers are strong enough not merely to admit difficulty but to analyse it. Often these are the young ones and yet the help they receive from their elders is often of the 'pocket cudgel' variety. There seems to be an inbuilt reliance upon anecdote as a response to the statement of a seriously felt problem. It's all rather like the behaviour of 'reps' who find themselves, friends for a night, in some fairly desolate two-star hotel: they spend their time capping each other's stories. It would be difficult to say whether they are more terrified of really saying something or of really listening.

It was as an attempt to break some new ground in this difficult area that some years ago Geoff Fox and I tried to devise for teachers on an in-service course in

Lancashire a situation or framework that would enable them not only to admit real difficulty, but also to listen properly to each other. The result of this was something we called, perhaps infelicitously, 'The Clinic'. The ground rules are simple.

1 There are five or six participants.
2 Each is asked in advance to formulate a statement of a real teaching problem. This could be deeply revealing (I don't like kids) or technical (I can't teach the full stop). The range of choice is made clear to them but it should be emphasized that the exercise is best left until late on in the course, when some confidence and trust have been established.
3 In turn, half an hour is devoted to each participant by the whole group. This is divided as follows
  (i) Participant states the nature of the problem (5–10 minutes allowed). No interruptions.
  (ii) The others question, to try to clarify the problem further, or help the speaker to do so (10 minutes).
  (iii) They then offer suggestions (10–15 minutes) based on what they have learnt. *Absolutely no anecdotes or personal illustrations are allowed.*
4 One member of the group, in turn, acts as chair and strict time-keeper and either the chair or another participant of the group takes careful note of the suggestions offered, since the person involved is too busy listening to do so, but is given these notes at the end.

This may sound like a particularly difficult sort of encounter group, but all those I have known who posed a significant problem came away heartened. Often these teachers had been working in near-impossible circumstances; the others, having listened, offered some help but the main encouragement came in the whole group telling them that they weren't in fact failing but putting up a bloody good show!

We would not want to make any extreme claims for this idea – for its originality, design or whatever. (I would indeed welcome suggestions for its improvement.) Nevertheless it appears to meet certain conditions: it breaks through at least the first level of unproductive defensiveness; it offers the support of a rule-bound, clear-cut (and relatively short) routine; and most importantly it offers a teacher with a problem the unprecedented experience of being *properly and patiently attended to* by five sympathetic colleagues. It could form a very useful element, I believe, in any residential course of about a week's duration or of a part-time course which runs long and regularly enough for mutual confidence to be built up. It is, however, unsuited to any courses – of which all too many lurk on the horizon – based on the premise that what teachers need is some kind of 'topping-up'.

Having offered just one possible tactic that starts with the teacher, two others of wider applicability suggest themselves. Both of these, in common with suggestions earlier in the book, owe a good deal more to therapeutic psychology than to linguistic or literary studies. The first is highly specific; the second is more general and indeed gives the context in which the first should be set.

From the world of counselling, teachers might do well to borrow the technique known in the trade as *reflecting*. A 'client' being counselled offers some halting, partial explanation of a particular predicament. The 'counsellor' responds by repeating a few of the client's key words and expressions. 'Reflecting' indeed has a double sense: not only is it at once 'reflecting back' almost like a verbal mirror, but also the way the client's words are received and echoed suggests that the counsellor is indeed reflecting and mulling them over. This is a signal of acceptance and encouragement, conveying the idea that the thoughts, however incomplete, merit the counsellor's attention. Crucially this technique offers time as well as encouragement; thus the client is enabled, possibly very slowly, to expand or reformulate ideas. It might not seem a particularly clever approach until you contrast it with a teacherly one – with responses that demand clarification, for example 'What on earth do you mean, boy?' 'Reflecting' demands great patience and self-restraint: the temptation to question, advise, interpret or suggest has to be resisted for a long time. Interestingly some techniques in English already suggested bear some resemblance to this – in spirit if not in detail. 'Conferencing' as Graves (1983) described it might work better for the conscious use of this technique, but his suggestions already emphasize the need for waiting – often for a painfully long time in the early stages – before moving on to questioning. In both situations teacher or counsellor have to recognize that the deeper the sense of inadequacy, the harder it will be for the pupil/client to think, let alone articulate these thoughts.

All of which leads naturally enough to Carl Rogers. In *On Becoming a Person* (1974) there is a section on 'breakdowns in communication' in which from his background in counselling and psychotherapy he presents two ideas. The first is the hypothesis

> that the major barrier to mutual interpersonal communication is our very natural tendency to judge, to evaluate, to approve or disapprove, the statement of the other person, or the other group . . .
>
> (Rogers 1974: 330)

After illustrating this idea with examples, Rogers offers a second proposition: that the seriousness of these judgemental blockages to real communication is proportional to the extent to which feelings or emotions are involved. Citing his clinical experience, he argues – in a way reminiscent of Martin Buber (1947) as quoted in Chapters 1 and 3 – that both problems may be solved by a systematic attempt to see, or feel, the other person's point of view, that is by empathetic understanding.

Feeling that his readers may remain sceptical or, more importantly perhaps, may retain a complacent confidence in their own listening capacities, Rogers offers them a kind of challenge: 'a little laboratory experiment' with which to 'test the quality of their understanding . . .'

> The next time you get into an argument with your wife, or your friend, or with a small group of friends, just stop the discussion for a moment and for an experiment, institute this rule. 'Each person can speak up for himself only after he has first restated the ideas and feelings of the previous speaker accurately, and to that speaker's satisfaction'. You see what this would mean. It would simply mean that before presenting your own point of view, it would be necessary for you to really achieve the other speaker's frame of reference – to understand his thoughts and feelings so well that you could summarize them for him. Sounds simple, doesn't it? But if you try it you will discover it is one of the most difficult things you have ever tried to do. However, once you have been able to see the other's point of view, your own comments will have to be drastically revised. You will also find the emotion going out of the discussion, the differences being reduced, and those differences which remain being of a rational and understandable sort.[14]
>
> (Rogers 1974: 330–3)

Before picking up on Rogers's attractive idea of conducting little experiments, and as we move towards a conclusion, it seems important to address a wider question: the relationship between teacher and therapist. I have sought throughout the book to emphasize what the former can learn from the practice of the latter but this is not to suggest that the roles are interchangeable. What the teacher can hope to learn is insight rather than healing skills.

This said, by their engagement with real life through literature and through the speaking and writing activities English teachers are called on to promote, they are bound to touch parts of children's inner lives. Indeed their function, as I have argued, is to help children explore and value their thinking and feeling processes. In this, if they are sensitive – or lucky – teachers may well set in train movements that have a healing quality. 'Treatment' however falls outside their scope.

Insights derived from therapy also seem particularly relevant to the current emphasis not merely on engineering situations but more specifically on the effective use of group work. In *Lost for Words* (1972) I outlined Carl Rogers's twin concepts of psychological safety and psychological freedom:[15] Rogers saw the establishment of *psychological safety* as depending on three conditions which had to be fulfilled if creativity was to be fostered:

1　The unconditional acceptance of the individual. Here the teacher, parent or therapist was called upon to sense and have faith in the potentialities of the individual.
2　The provision of an unthreatening 'climate' in which the individual, unburdened by constant external evaluation, could move towards greater self-acceptance and, ultimately, self-evaluation.
3　Empathetic understanding, where the adult concerned strives to enter into the other's point of view, and hence give him or her permission to allow his or her 'real self to emerge'.

Psychological freedom was Rogers's term for describing conditions which allowed the individual 'a complete freedom of symbolic expression' thus fostering 'the openness, and the playful and spontaneous juggling of percepts, concepts and meanings'. This stress on playfulness and its attendant 'juggling' is directly in line with my thesis throughout this book, as indeed is his emphasis on the 'climate' in which such things can be made possible.

As I recognized in *Lost for Words* the kind of acceptance of which Rogers speaks is hard to achieve or even approach. None the less, if we are trying to interest children in the workings of their own minds, we have at least to move tenaciously in this direction. And we have to do so in an educational climate which appears intoxicated with 'assessment' and which not merely looks unfavourably on therapeutic considerations but where politicians encourage a kind of thinking which draws its imagery more from the world of commercial competition than from education. This is nowhere more clearly seen than in the current obsession with courses apparently designed to prove to 'senior management' that what they are 'running' is more like a sausage factory than what I would recognize as a school.

More recently, the development of Local Management of Schools and of open enrolment has served to accelerate the replacement of educational values and procedures by those of the market place. There, as we have been told frequently in recent years, competition and choices are key criteria of success. Unfortunately, as educators have known for a long time, some are better placed to compete than others while there are also many for whom 'choice' is not an option. It is distressing to those who care about schools and children to observe headteachers being forced to adopt tactics more appropriate to the competition of rival departmental stores. This issue was recently addressed directly by Cardinal Hume at the North of England education conference:

> I believe that the fostering of competition among schools and the introduction of commercial concepts is on undesirable and dangerous development. We need to be aware that competitive markets always create losers, and as a society we cannot afford to allow any schools which meet a local need to lose out. If we do, we are damaging the pupils at those schools, the education they should have and which it is within our power to provide.[16]

The merest reference to therapy as in some way relevant to teaching would be sufficient to convince these new educational industrialists that I belong to some woolly minded (green?) 'developmental' party rather than to those who have the realism to recognize the need for skills. I have never undervalued this need – but have placed the first emphasis on the conditions which direct experience and observation have convinced me are necessary if these skills are to be acquired. Equally I have never thought that the apprentice woodworker is greatly helped by being given heaps of wood but never being shown how to use saw or chisel. On the contrary, when skills are introduced at appropriate times or in appropriate contexts, they are a means towards growth: not only do they improve language but also they improve the quality of thinking and feeling.

I am indebted to my old friend and colleague, David Evans, who pointed out the need to clarify my position on these issues. Having read the manuscript in draft he also posed the question, 'What kind of child did I want to see emerging from the classroom?' I hope that the answer may be explicit or implicit in most of what has been already said – the belief in processes which encourage children to think, to question, and to be increasingly confident about their mental processes, particularly as these relate to expression through language.

To David's question should perhaps be added another integral to the purposes of this book: 'What kind of teachers do I want to see entering the classroom?' The emphasis on learning from therapy has at least as much to do with them as with those in their charge. Given the pressures to which they are currently subject, they too have a need for healing, the kind which leads to a clearer recognition of and deeper valuing of themselves and their own inner processes. In the current climate and with inadequate and erratic provision for in-service training, such needs seem likely to suffer protracted neglect. Certainly the need for a sustaining core of belief was never greater than now. Despite this I remain, hopeful for, unlike Shaw, I believe that most teachers are not merely hard-working but astonishingly inventive when they receive the right kind of encouragement.

When this condition is fulfilled they will be perpetually trying 'little experiments', of the kind suggested by Carl Rogers, in order to improve communication and enhance thinking, across the whole field of English.

To conclude: the needs of teacher and taught are not so different. Certainly the child within each teacher needs cherishing; and the teacher's willingness to engage in experiments large or small will always depend on being in communication with the child *inside* as well as meeting the challenges posed by children outside. As Albert Cullum put it

Teacher, come on outside!
I'll race you to the seesaw!
No, you won't fall off!
I'll show you how!
Don't be afraid, teacher.
Grab my hand and follow me.
You can learn all over again! . . .[17]

Which is perhaps where real teaching starts.

Notes

1 'Coleridge's Table Talk, 1819–23', reported in Stephen Potter (ed.) (1933) *Coleridge*, Nonesuch Press, p. 477.
2 For an early formulation of these ideas see Creber (1965) *Sense and Sensitivity*, University of London Press, pp. 30–1 and 51–2 (or 24–5 and 48–9 in the revised

edition, 1983, School of Education, University of Exeter). The discussion which follows here draws on later formulations, three articles in particular: 'Voiceless Poems 1' and 'Voiceless Poems 2', in *Language for Learning*, June 1979, vol. 1, nos 2 and 3, School of Education, University of Exeter; and 'Look and Learn or Learn to Look', in *Perspectives 20: What are English Teachers for?*, 1985, School of Education, University of Exeter.

3 *Reflections* (1963) compiled by S. Clements, J. Dickson and L. Stratta, Oxford: Oxford University Press.

4 M. Benton (1989) *The First Two Rs*, Department of Education, University of Southampton.

5 *Story Boards* and *Teacher's Guide* by Olivia W. Hill (1967) were originally published in the USA by Houghton Mifflin and published in the UK by ESA Creative Learning, Harlow, Essex.

6 For example, see A. D. Edwards (1976) 'Speech codes and speech variants; social class and task differences in children's speech', *Journal of Child Language* 3, no. 2.

7 On collage see also Purves *et al.* (1972) pp. 133–5.

8 G. Fox and B. Merrick (1985) 'The mind's eye', in *Perspectives 20: What are English Teachers for?* School of Education, University of Exeter.

9 Roger Fry (1937) *Vision and Design*, Harmondsworth: Pelican, quoted in Rod Taylor (1986) *Educating for Art*, London: Longman.

10 A. Cullum (1971) *The Geranium on the Window Sill Just Died but Teacher You Went Right On*, New York: Harlin Quist.

11 Kahlil Gibran (1978) *The Prophet*, Heinemann, London, p. 54 (Originally published 1923).

12 C. Sutton *et al.* (1981) *Communicating in the Classroom*, London: Hodder & Stoughton, p. 80.

13 Cullum op. cit.

14 A rather simpler version of this little experiment is given among the suggestions in *Communicating in the Classroom*.

15 See Rogers (1974) pp. 301 and 357–8.

16 Cardinal Hume, quoted in *The Times* (1990) 'Cardinal launches wide attack on education reforms', 4 January.

17 Cullum op. cit.

Appendix
Ninety things to do with a picture*

What follows is a compilation of ideas produced by PGCE students and practising teachers over a number of years. Inevitably there is some overlap but this seems unimportant: the purpose of the list is to give an idea of the range of possibilities and to generate new ideas.

Character-based tasks

1 *Dossier on character*
   Choose one person in the picture. Compile a dossier on him/her. (Family tree, likes/dislikes, career, history, important events etc.)
2 *'What's My Line'*
   Guess the specific work a character might do to make him/her special.
3 *Obituary*
   Write an obituary for the character depicted.
4 *Diary*
   Write a diary for this character.
5 *Character study*
   A character in the picture applies for a job you have advertised. Would you employ him/her?
6 *Character study*
   Write a description and character study of the *exact opposite* of the character in the picture.
7 *Character study*
   Write an imaginative account of one of the characters shown in the picture. What is he/she like as a person?
8 *Character study*
   Do you trust the character? Imagine he/she is trying to do a deal with you. Write a dialogue of the encounter. Would you buy a used car from him/her?
9 *'This is Your Life'*
   Select and write dramatically about events which would feature in this character's *This is Your Life*.

*Originally published in Creber, J. W. P. (1985) 'What are English teachers for?' *Perspectives*, 20, University of Exeter School of Education.

10 *Animal Associations*
What animal reminds you of this character and why? People often look like their dogs. Can you write an amusing description about an animal and its owner? With illustrations.

11 *Fiction*
A character reminds you of a character in a poem/play/novel. Which and why?

12 *Stereotypes*
Do these characters remind you of any stereotype characters/images. If so, explain!

13 *Questions*
The photograph gives you clues to this character's identity. You have to find out about him/her by asking questions. What questions would you ask?

14 *Interview*
Write an interview with this character. What do you want to know about him/her?

15 *Computer dating*
Write a description of this person's character for a computer-dating questionnaire. Find the right type of person to match with your character and write a biography for him/her.

16 *Disguise*
The character is in disguise. What is his/her true identity and what is the reason for the disguise?

17 *7, 14, 21*
What was the person in the picture like at 7, 14 and 21 years old?

18 *Fancy dress*
Write an amusing invitation to a fancy dress party for this person. What would he/she come as and why? Describe his/her appearance in fancy dress.

19 *Black sheep*
Imagine this person as the black sheep of the family. Give his/her mother's account of his/her misdeeds.

20 *Life history*
Give a life history of this character – you could predict a life history of a younger person.

21 *Memory loss*
The character shown is suffering from amnesia – try and establish his/her true identity.

22 *'I used to be'*
'I used to be . . . but now I . . .' What did the character used to be? What has happened, and how, to change his/her life?

23 *Viewpoints*
You are the character depicted. How would you react in a given situation as that character?

Visual composition

A pupil (group of pupils) is given a photograph with the question/task:

24 You are the photographer – explain why you took this picture. What were you trying to say? What effects were you using?

25 Using a selection of pictures cut out from magazines/newspapers etc. build up a pictorial composition/document (no words allowed).

26 Wanted poster – design a 'wanted' poster for a character depicted.

27 Build up a collage using pictures and words from magazines/newspapers; drawings with a theme in mind e.g. myself, my town, a particular poem, story, theme in a story.

28 What could this picture *advertise?*
29 Draw a map of the surrounding countryside, given the scene in the photo.
30 (i) Design a book cover for a book you have read incorporating title, front picture, blurb, spine.
   (ii) What book could this picture illustrate?
   (iii) Cut out pictures to form a book cover.
31 Why do you think this photograph was taken?
32 Show a series of pictures rapidly – what pictures stay in mind and why?
33 'Pictorial close' – leave a block of a picture out (cut out a square).
34 'Creative arts' – turn the picture into a cartoon, and use it as first or last frame in a picture story.
35 Given this picture of a face, describe the rest of the body.
36 One person, from close observation of the photo, has to describe it in detail to someone who has to draw it. Compare the result with the original. How could it be improved?
37 What films or TV programmes does this picture remind you of?
38 As if in the *TV Times*, write the parts for a programme to go with this photograph.
39 Select a series of photographs that could make up a slide show, i.e. one theme. Give a commentary to accompany the show.
40 'Postcard' – use the photograph as an unusual postcard. Write an appropriate text.
41 'Obstruction'
   (i) What problems are posed by the viewing of a picture of oneself? *Alice Through the Looking Glass*.
   (ii) The view of a scene with reference to a time never to be experienced – perhaps to go with a reading of Keats's 'Ode on a Grecian Urn'. What separates us from the scene behind the glaze?

Descriptive and factual tasks

42 Devise a travel brochure advertising the delights and appeal of the place in the picture.
43 Using a picture of any sort of property, give an estate agent's description of this place. The task can be serious or a parody of a 'selling' style.
44 You are an explorer and consequently the first person to discover the landscape in the picture. Write a report describing it and give the location a name.
45 In groups, or pairs, write a paragraph on a particular photo individually. Compare your results. Why did you latch onto particular features?
46 Describe a walk through this photo of a particular landscape.
47 The photograph shows a particular scene in a particular season. Describe the same scene in a different season.
48 This photo has been taken from a newspaper. Devise a headline and article to accompany it.
49 Write an insect-eye view of the scene in the picture.
50 Describe the home of the character in the picture.
51 What does the rest of the area look like, judging from the evidence of the picture?
52 Use a picture of recreational or spare-time activity to act as stimulus for discussion of writing about out of school activities.
53 Discuss the relative values of different forms of pictures to perform different tasks, e.g. advertising, road signs, paintings.

Letters

54 Using the picture as your starting point, write a letter to an aunt thanking her for this unusual gift.

55 Write a letter from the person(s) in the picture to someone of your choice.
56 Write a love/hate letter to or from the person(s) in the picture.

Making music

57 Choose four pictures then select a suitable piece of music to go with each.
58 Choose songs or pieces of music to illustrate a picture or vice versa.
59 Make up a sound track to accompany this picture.
60 Describe or put on tape background sounds to accompany this picture.

Drama

61 Make a tableau of the picture and follow it through. What happened before you froze the picture? What happened after?
62 Interview two or three people involved in a crowd scene picture. They give an eye-witness account of what they are watching (i.e. an event).
63 Would you take the person in the picture home as a potential boy/girl friend? With a partner improvise a scene:
    (i) father/mother
    (ii) son/daughter
    Opening line: 'Mum/Dad I've got a picture of my boy/girl friend. What do you think?'
64 Write a dialogue between characters in the picture.

Games

65 What is the first word that comes into your head when you have seen this picture? Quickfire/brainstorms/associations/lists.
66 'Stream of consciousness' – jot down any random thoughts that the picture suggests.
67 Write down statements about the picture. Now write them backwards. Swap with a friend. Make up your own simple code and clues and others try and find out what the picture was about.
68 For one minute talk about the picture without deviation, hesitation or repetition.
69 'Kim's game' – remember as much detail as possible after the picture has been taken away.
70 Write a list of adjectives suitable for this picture.
71 One person has the photograph/picture. The others in the group have 20 questions to find out what it is.
72 Pretend you are an expert on this picture. Tell the class about it.
73 'Alphabet game' – using a picture, list all the objects etc. beginning with 'A' – then 'B/C/' etc. Could lead to exploration of mood?
74 Write down eight things that are true about this picture, then deliberately write down an opposite to your chosen words/objects. Let the group find out what was depicted in the picture.
75 Compose captions for a series of photographs.
76 'Wordsquare' – construct a wordsearch based on this picture.

Stories

77 This character has disappeared. You were the last person to see him/her. What has happened?
78 You hear a voice telling you the story behind the picture. What does it say?

79 Use this photo to write a ghost story.
80 A day in the life – write an imaginative account of *one* day in the life of a person shown in the picture. What would he/she do on an average day?
81 What would happen if you went home and found this character waiting for you? Write a story/poem/play.
82 What would the person in this picture do if they won £500,000?
83 This person did a most remarkable thing for the town. What was it?
84 This picture is part of a dream. Give an account of the whole dream.
85 The teacher uncovers the picture bit by bit. The class predict and describe what the whole picture might be and write the story behind it.

Poems

86 Mood – establish the mood of the photo. Each member of the group writes one line, then they compile them to form a poem.
87 Study the picture, then write down sentences about it, each sentence containing as many words beginning with the same letters as you can, to make an alliterative poem.
88 Write a limerick which this picture illustrates.
89 Pick one word that describes the picture or sums it up, and use it as the basis for acrostics poem about the picture.
90 Use the picture as a basis for the lyrics of a song.

Bibliography

Balaam, J. and Merrick, B. (1987) *Exploring Poetry 5 to 8*, Exeter: A. Wheaton for NATE.

Barnes, D. (1976) *From Communication to Curriculum*, Harmondsworth: Penguin.

Benton, M. and Fox, G. (1985) *Teaching Literature, Nine to Fourteen*, Oxford University Press.

Britton, J. (1970) *Language and Learning*, Harmondsworth: Penguin.

Britton, J. *et al.* (1975) *The Development of Writing Abilities*, London: Macmillan.

Brownjohn, S. (1980) *Does it Have to Rhyme?*, London: Hodder & Stoughton.

— (1982) *What Rhymes with Secret?*, London: Hodder & Stoughton.

Buber, M. (1947) *Between Man and Man*, London: Collins/Fontana.

Bullock Report (1975) *A Language for Life*, London: HMSO.

Buzan, T. (1974) *Use your Head*, London: BBC Books.

Cox Report (1988) *English for Ages 5–11*, London: DES.

— (1989) *English for Ages 5–16*, London: DES.

Creber, J. W. P. (1965) *Sense and Sensitivity*, University of London Press; revised edition (1983) School of Education, Exeter University.

— (1972) *Lost for Words*, Harmondsworth: Penguin; (1974) Bristol Classical Press.

Cullum, A. (1971) *The Geranium on the Window Sill Just Died but Teacher You Went Right On*, New York: Harlin Quist.

Dixon, J. (1975) *Growth through English*, Oxford University Press, for NATE.

Elbow, P. (1973) *Writing Without Teachers*, New York: Oxford University Press.

Graves, D. (1983) *Writing*, London: Heinemann.

Hackman, S. (1987) *Responding in Writing*, Exeter: Short Run Press for NATE.

Holmes, E. (1911) *What is and What might be*, London: Constable.

Hourd, M. L. (1949) *The Education of the Poetic Spirit*, London: Heinemann.

Hughes, T. (1967) *Poetry in the Making*, London: Faber.

James, W. (1947) 'On a certain blindness in human beings', in *Selected Papers on Philosophy*, London: Everyman.

Jones, R. (1968) *Feeling and Fantasy in Education*, University of London Press.

Kingman Report (1988) *Report on the Committee of Enquiry into the Teaching of English Language*, London: HMSO.

Koch, K. (1970) *Wishes, Lies, and Dreams*, New York: Chelsea House.

Langer, S. (1957) *Philosophy in a New Key*, Cambridge, Mass: Harvard University Press.

Lunzer, E. and Gardner, K. (eds) (1979) *The Effective Use of Reading*, London: Heinemann.

Maslow, A. M. (1961) *Towards a Psychology of Being*, New York: Van Nostrand.

Milner, M. (1971) *On Not Being Able to Paint*, London: Heinemann.

Moffett, J. (1968) *Teaching the University of Discourse*, Boston, Mass: Houghton Mifflin.

Newbolt Report (1921) *The Teaching of English in England*, London: HMSO.

Purves, A. C. (ed.) (1972) *How Porcupines Make Love*, Lexington, Mass: Xerox College Publishing.

Rogers, C. (1974) *On Becoming a Person*, London: Constable.

Rosen, H. and Rosen, C. (1973) *The Language of Primary School Children*, Harmondsworth: Penguin.

Sampson, G. (1921) *English for the English*, Cambridge University Press.

Winnicott, D. W. (1971) *Playing and Reality*, London: Tavistock.

Witkin, R. W. (1974) *The Intelligence of Feeling*, London: Heinemann Educational Books.